Praise for TOX

Many people assume that toxicity is somet
er people and "happens to us." It is, howev
on ourselves owing to the way we view and
control.

The only emotions we can truly control are our own and this book helps us understand how to manage our own triggers, emotions and toxicity before addressing those of others.

Once we have grasped this essential truth, we are well armed to learn the strategies to adopt to handle the various types and degrees of toxicity we encounter, in the workplace, with relationships and with the frustrations of modern life.

Toxicum explains all of this and more besides, and the 'case studies' detail situations that many of us will be able to relate to. A wonderful, highly readable and entertaining book, full of wisdom.

—Prof Bud Drago, Professor of Marketing at Villanova University

"*Toxicum: Managing Toxic People* is a fascinating and inspiring read, full of excellent advice for managing one of the most difficult and stressful aspects of life, the toxic individual. Toxic people are one of the greatest sources of anxiety, dysfunction and unhappiness and are to be found, regrettably, in all walks of life, from the boardroom to the bedroom. They also come in many guises. No-one is immune to their threat. This book is timely and highly educative, explaining the many techniques used by the toxic person and then providing very practical strategies to counter them. The case studies in the last part, taken from real events, are especially enlightening, covering, as they do, many different situations. Highly recommended!'"

—Jean Fleming PCC, Empowerment and Leadership Coach, Program Director 'Women in Leadership' and former board director of Atos SE

However inspired, motivated, strong and enthusiastic we may be, individually and collectively, it is inevitable that, sooner or later, we will be faced, in our personal or business life, with a toxic person or people.

Toxic people can poison relationships, destroy harmony and generate stress in almost any and all situations, unless they are correctly confronted, countered and managed. That's why *Toxicum: Managing Toxic People* is so timely and so valuable. The book describes the nature of Toxicity is in detail, challenges the reader to examine their own toxicity and provides strategies which are highly practical and illustrated in a variety of case studies drawn from the authors' own experience. *Toxicum: Managing Toxic People,* is a wonderful book, easy to read and full of enlightening and usable advice. It addresses brilliantly the very important problem of toxicity, the cause of so much anxiety and misery. A 'must read' for anyone wanting to manage toxicity and restore peace and balance to their life, and those of their family, friends and work colleagues. Vernon and Katey fully understand the challenges we all face in dealing with toxicity. Their words of wisdom and sound advice will stay with me always.

—Joy Atkinson, President and CEO at Presperse Inc.

Toxicum is a highly readable and well-written book, with an abundance of good, practical advice. Sankey and Lockwood do a masterful job of explaining toxicity and its origins, and of providing strategies for dealing with its many manifestations. Their guidance on understanding and managing one's own toxicity is enlightening, and their case studies illustrating how to apply their strategies are spot on. I strongly recommend *Toxicum* to anyone wanting to free themselves from the suffering and stress that toxic people create. Readers will come away much better equipped to confront toxicity whenever it rears its ugly head."

—Lynn S. Paine, Baker Foundation Professor, John G. McLean Professor of Business Administration Emerita, Harvard Business School

TOXICUM

Managing Toxic People

Vernon Sankey** and **Katey Lockwood

Improve Your World

ISBN: 978-1-8384114-2-8 (softcover)
ISBN: 978-1-8384114-3-5 (ebook)

Improve Your World Publishers Co Limited
www.improvemyworld.com

Book design by Jill Ronsley, suneditwrite.com

Printed and bound in the United Kingdom

Contents

Introduction

One of the most difficult and stress-inducing phenomena human beings can endure is toxicity—our own as well as that of others. This book is designed to give understanding and guidance on this vital area of our lives.

When Jean-Paul Sartre wrote *'L'enfer, c'est les autres'* ('Hell is other people') he was referring, among other things, to the innate toxicity of human beings and their interrelationships. Everything would be so easy if it were not for other people!

We all know what toxicity means, but what makes toxicity so difficult to understand and manage is that it comes in so many forms—from very subtle to overtly narcissistic, and everything in between.

As a result, no single approach or strategy will necessarily work. What makes it even trickier is that toxicity is all about emotions rather than logic, defying clear categorization or simple intellectual analysis. Self-awareness, self-confidence, assertiveness, interpersonal skills and empathy, all of which are not easy to master and have little to do with intellectual logic, are the appropriate personal key attributes to develop and use to address this most painful of human issues.

To face the problems and challenges of human toxicity means to understand, empathize and appreciate deeply the feelings, emotions and energy of human beings and their interactions at their most intense and impassioned.

As Dale Carnegie wrote:

> When dealing with people, let us remember we are not dealing with creatures of logic. We are dealing with creatures of emotion, creatures bristling with prejudice and motivated by pride and vanity.

Toxicity is the cause of much unhappiness and heartbreak, suffering and despair, anxiety and mental and physical health problems. Sometimes the toxic person is aware of their toxicity, sometimes not. Whatever their own intentions or self-awareness, the results are painful in the extreme for their victims. Make no mistake. Toxicity kills.

In the words of Bryant McGill:

> Toxic relationships are dangerous for your health; they will literally kill you. Stress shortens your lifespan. Even a broken heart can kill you. There is an undeniable mind-body connection. Your arguments and hateful talk can land you in the emergency room or in the morgue. You were not meant to live in a fever of anxiety; screaming yourself hoarse in a frenzy of dreadful panicked fight-or-flight that leaves you exhausted and numb with grief.

Life is not meant to be lived like this and no one should be subjected to this suffering. Nor is there any need to do so. With awareness, discipline and understanding you can deal with this all too common and savage phenomenon.

Toxicum explores and analyses the background to toxicity and its various manifestations. It explores why and how toxicity occurs and offers suggestions on how to address toxic people and toxic situations when they arise.

We believe *Toxicum* is unique. We offer guides and pointers on how to deal with toxicity based on both Western psychology *and* Eastern philosophical and psychological teachings. As a result, the subject is covered from more perspectives. We also examine both the toxicity we experience and the one we project—our own personal toxicity—and the extent to which we are both willing and unwitting accessories in this process.

Both West and East arrive at many of the same conclusions regarding best practice, but they do so from very different standpoints. It is through understanding both approaches that the best learnings will occur.

The teachings of this book are of course wholly compatible with the lifestyle and personal transformation guidance of our previous work:

> *The Way: Finding Peace in Turbulent Times* (Sankey and Lockwood, 2019)
>
> *The Way Workbook* (Sankey and Lockwood, 2021)
>
> *The Stairway to Happiness* (Sankey, 2018)

How to Use This Book

If you are reading this book, or even just browsing its contents out of curiosity, you are almost certainly wondering what you can do about a toxic person or situation. What should you do next time you find yourself with a toxic individual? How can you change a toxic relationship that is always influencing you? How could you handle an unpleasant encounter better? Or how could you help someone else who is in a toxic situation?

While it is easy to find general information about toxicity in books, and especially online, in *Toxicum* we take a unique approach to freeing you from toxicity so that you can live the life you deserve. Our approach is based on extensive research and experience.

In **Part 1: Understanding Toxicity**, we use tools gathered from different fields—social, psychological and spiritual, along with lots of practical implementations—to show you how to recognize the many forms of toxicity and their causes.

We begin in chapter 1 by defining toxicity, which helps to focus on the issue in ways that go beyond its colloquial usage and prepares the ground for genuinely addressing the problem. Chapter 2, 'How to Recognize Toxicity', goes into much greater detail and provides an extensive checklist to pinpoint toxic behaviour.

Toxicity arises largely from unexamined causes and in chapter 3 we begin to outline what these might be (each case being unique in its details). We believe it is impossible to understand and, more importantly, be free from toxicity unless the *role of ego* is properly grasped. This false sense of who we are (ironically) lacks self-awareness and cannot be empathetic. What we experience as a toxic situation is invariably the ego playing out past patterns with no regard for others.

We conclude the 'defining' chapters of Part 1 with chapter 4, which focuses on toxicity where many of us suffer it most badly—the workplace.

We then come to the most crucial and perhaps unexpected point. In general parlance, toxicity is always something that *other people* exhibit and *we* suffer from. However, one of the most important lessons from our research and practice has been that we cannot eliminate toxicity apparently caused by others if we do not address it in ourselves first!

Examining our personal role and responsibility in the creation and resolution of toxic situations forms the backbone of Part 1 (in chapters 5–7). This is tough work and we do not attempt to disguise the fact. We provide techniques drawn from different disciplines (notably the 'shadow work' of Jung in chapter 7) to look at ourselves honestly.

Why do we emphasize this? Because only by looking deeply within can we learn how to regain power over ourselves and our reactions in different situations. This is the message of chapters 8 and 9. Only by learning to manage our own toxicity—and thus know ourselves more completely—will we be able to properly address the toxicity of others and live a happier, more fulfilling life.

Once we have assimilated the foundational learnings of Part 1, we move on to **Part 2: Key Strategies**. There are 7 Key Strategies to deal with toxic people and situations and each is explained in depth. Through their use, usually in combination and over time, we believe that you will be able to free yourself from any form of toxicity.

We begin with how to avoid getting embroiled in the first place (Key Strategy 1). Since this is often very difficult or impossible, such as with family members, Key Strategies 2–6 cover how best to act.

We must be *masters of our own reactions* (Key Strategy 2), be able to *stay calm* (Key Strategy 3) and *interact assertively* (Key Strategy 5). At the same time, learning how to *set boundaries* (Key Strategy 4) is crucial, especially in ongoing situations.

If at all possible, we want to resolve the situation, which is where Key Strategy 6 comes in. With the firm base given by the previous Key Strategies, we are in a strong position to *focus on solutions.*

Our final strategy (Key Strategy 7) concentrates on *building great relationships.* These not only help us avoid toxicity, but also give us the support we need should a negative situation arise.

In Parts 3 and 4, the focus shifts to practical examples.

Part 3: Common Toxic Types describes four sets of character traits that can be extremely toxic: cynically negative; ungrateful and mean; responsibility averse; and the interpersonally flawed, hypersensitive and humourless. We analyse each type and show how and which combination of the Key Strategies can be used to counter their negativity.

Part 4: Case Studies covers real-world examples in depth. We describe actual events and how the Key Strategies were employed to resolve negative situations. While each case is very specific, there are many lessons we can draw from each one and aspects of them that will feel very familiar. You may wish to start by reading a particular case study that speaks to you. We have given each one a generic title, such as the 'Toxic Partner', to aid you.

Toxicum concludes with two important appendices that we believe will be of value at all times.

Appendix 1: The Importance and Value of Meditation outlines how meditative practice helps us understand ourselves and toxicity, while providing many health and wellbeing benefits. We outline an easy-to-follow practice with insights of meditation in Western and Eastern traditions.

Appendix 2: Quick Checklist for Toxic Emergencies is a summary of the 7 Key Strategies for dealing with toxicity. Hopefully, you will not have to employ this too frequently, but we felt it was worth including the heart of the book in a simple and easy-to-use form. Having read the preceding chapters will make this appendix particularly useful.

Freeing yourself from toxicity is one of the most valuable things you can do and the key to a fulfilling, worthwhile life. We hope that all that we have learned, experienced, researched and shared in *Toxicum* will help you.

PART 1

Understanding Toxicity

1

What Is Toxicity?

The word itself comes from the Latin word *toxicum* meaning 'poisoned', which, in turn, comes from the Greek word for the poison that was spread on arrows. It means 'extremely harsh', 'malicious', 'harmful', 'deadly'. And these meanings are no understatements.

We use 'toxicity' to describe a situation or person that is 'poisonous' to our health and wellbeing. Like all poisons, they can be life threatening. Poisons are best avoided. But if this is not possible, then it is best to understand what type of poison we are faced with and apply an antidote as quickly and effectively as possible.

How to successfully manage 'toxic' people is one of the most difficult interpersonal challenges we face. It's also one of the most important to master. Whether in the workplace, at home, or with any relationships, toxicity results in feeling misunderstood, demeaned, ignored, unsupported, unloved or abused. Toxicity is likely to occur whenever our safety, wellbeing or enjoyment of life is threatened, whether emotionally, psychologically or physically.

Toxic situations are those in which we feel uncomfortable, judged, distrusted, disrespected, criticised or unvalued. They can occur anywhere, from the boardroom to the bedroom, from the playing field to the pub, and everywhere in between. Any time we feel worse rather than better after an exchange, we are in the presence of some level of toxicity.

Toxic people come in many guises. They can be overtly aggressive and obnoxious or subtly manipulative and controlling. Some people become toxic on specific occasions, triggered by a condition (for example, drunkenness), a perceived slight, a disparaging comment, being ignored, feeling unvalued or unloved, criticised or denied. Others are more permanently angry and argumentative, seething and vengeful and even psychopathically needing to control and cause pain in a futile attempt to relieve their own self-loathing. They have been conditioned to see the world as a negative place in which survival depends on the destruction of others. There is no room for sympathy or empathy for others in their lives. Ego and their own false sense of who they think they are have completely taken over.

Toxic people can appear very confident or very timid. In reality, the 'mask' worn conceals a chronic lack of self-awareness and self-confidence, leading to a total absence of sensitivity, compassion or love.

Toxicity is almost always directly related to some past trauma (or traumas) that have caused the toxic person to develop a mindset that reflects their inherently low self-worth. This mindset has evolved to include anger, envy and resentment. The absence of love, appreciation and respect endured early in life is then projected on to others, especially those caught in their manipulative net. Toxicity becomes part of their habitual behaviour pattern. Others suffer the same indignities and miseries that they themselves have experienced.

Are toxic people born or created? Nature or nurture? This is a discussion that goes back centuries. One theory is that 'nature' is the prime cause of toxicity: people are born with antisocial personality issues that lead to toxic behaviours. More recently, scientists have examined people with antisocial personality disorders (ASPD) using MRIs. These studies have revealed abnormalities in areas of the brain (the superior temporal gyrus) responsible for language processing and social cognition. Other studies of ASPD have found lower levels of certain enzymes that balance the emotions in the amygdala and hippocampus. Evidence also exists that genetics play a significant role in characteristics such as EQ (emotional quotient), IQ, alcoholism, social behaviour and sexual identity.

'Nurture' theories are based on the premise that the mind is born as a blank state, or tabula rasa. It is environmental factors that create most of the psychological and behavioural dysfunctionalities of toxicity. This was certainly the view of Aristotle (*De Anima*), the Stoic school, St Thomas Aquinas, John Locke (*Essay Concerning Human Understanding*) and, of course, Sigmund Freud. Freud believed fervently that human personalities are determined almost entirely by family dynamics (such as by the Oedipus complex) and the way a person is brought up.

There is no doubt that environmental issues are a major factor in the development of toxicity. The way children are raised and educated, and their early experience of life, is highly significant. It is well known that children who grow up in uncaring, unloving and abusive households are more likely to develop aggressive, antisocial, violent, erratic and potentially criminal behaviours. Such children are less likely to form meaningful, lasting, fulfilled or loving relationships.

Conversely, children who grow up in loving households where they are encouraged, challenged and guided by role-model parents are more likely to be balanced psychologically and become, in turn, role models for their children and for society as a whole. Similarly, at school, children with teachers who are open and honest and who inspire them to learn, read and use their imagination reap the benefits.

> Imagination is more important than knowledge. For knowledge is limited whereas imagination embraces the entire world, stimulating progress, giving birth to evolution.
>
> —Albert Einstein, interview, 1929

These are, of course, broad generalisations. There are many examples of wonderful people leading exemplary lives in spite of suffering the worst of starts. Equally there are examples of people displaying appallingly toxic behaviour in spite of, seemingly, the best possible care, support and education in childhood. It remains clear, however, that toxicity develops early in life and is closely linked to experiences encountered and confronted along the way.

Whatever the background reason for their toxicity, toxic people are highly skilled at targeting and attracting similar, vulnerable people. These 'victim mentality' types have also suffered and come to assume that such behaviour is normal. Misery attracts misery.

Toxic people are to be found in every walk of life: in business, media, sports, politics, the military, the public and private sector, communities, societies. They are also family members, partners, neighbours and friends.

They are skilled manipulators and very self-serving. Not only are they insensitive to their impact on those around them, but they also do not really care as long as their own needs are met. Their main objective is to enhance and bolster their own overinflated ego and look after number one. Whatever they project to the outside world, they are in fact constantly needing to compensate for their own low self-esteem and self-confidence. They seek ego security at any cost.

Also, some gain perverse satisfaction from causing pain and suffering, almost as a relief to themselves. They suffer and do not wish to suffer alone. Finding and having a hapless victim acts as a palliative. Often, they will project their negative feelings on to others simply to unload and vent their frustration and anger. Their ego needs boosting and they find it easiest to achieve this at the expense of someone else.

Ego needs regular 'feeding', which means finding fodder in the form of victims. People, especially those who are very sensitive, sympathetic and empathetic and have themselves suffered from previous abusive treatment, are particularly vulnerable and need to be especially wary.

2

How to Recognize Toxicity

Signs that we are in the presence of toxicity

It is important to distinguish between normal disagreements and toxicity. Disagreeing and holding different views is not only normal in good interpersonal relationships, but an essential ingredient. It helps in building rapport and friendships, developing deeper understanding of complex matters, learning, broadening the mind and acquiring experience. It is a vital part of human development.

Debate and discussion are healthy and desirable. We learn best by exposing different points of view openly and then discussing and testing them thoroughly. We do not need to be right or wrong. Being human means being able, uniquely among living species, to weigh up alternatives and make up our own mind. If we all agreed on everything, life would become exceedingly dull, progress would be very slow and then grind to a halt.

> We don't get harmony when everybody sings the same note. Only notes that are different can harmonize. The same is true with people.
>
> —Anonymous

Disagreements between people expressing opinions, when both parties genuinely listen to the opinion of the other in a desire to understand and learn, are immensely enriching. This is what makes the world evolve positively, encourages constructive challenges and stimulates creativity. It is also what raises the level of consciousness as we discover the beauty, richness and immensity of life and the universe itself.

When people express differences of views, it is also an immensely important occasion to show respect and genuine care by listening 'actively'. Active listening means where attention is focussed entirely on the speaker. It requires being in the moment. Active listening creates and deepens good relationships and has the added benefit of improving health and wellbeing. Such occasions are opportunities to demonstrate that another person is valued and affirmed, and that what they say matters. It is also a wonderful way to learn and share enriching and different perspectives.

Genuinely open communication, and the willingness to listen carefully to the thoughts, ideas, feelings and emotions of another, is a sign that a relationship is strong and mutually constructive. It builds rapport—an important antidote to toxicity.

In the words of the Prayer of Saint Francis:

> Grant that I may not so much seek to be consoled as to console; to be understood as to understand.

More recently, Stephen Covey, in his book *The Seven Habits of Highly Effective People*, wrote: 'Seek first to understand, then to be understood,'—a vital maxim for leadership.

While genuine communication is an indication of a strong relationship, the opposite is also true. It does not say much about a relationship if the expression of a different point of view results in defensiveness, argument, anger, withdrawal and a general falling-out. Genuine concerns and differences are feelings that are important to share and be open about.

When this happens, especially on a regular basis, we are clearly in the presence of some level of toxicity. Whenever there is resistance, there is ego. And whenever there is ego, there is the potential for toxicity.

An exchange of views with a toxic person in which the toxic person feels criticized or denied, will easily deteriorate. It will become a contest, a battle of wits and a win/lose conflict. In such negatively charged exchanges, there is no listening and little opportunity for constructive learning or progress. When this happens it is no longer about exploring differences for mutual benefit or any chance of learning, but a state of destructive warfare. One party must 'win' and the other 'lose', but, in reality, both parties have clearly lost.

What happens in this scenario is that the toxic person either reacts abruptly to some perceived slight or randomly provokes or launches an attack on another. The attacked person neither anticipates nor wishes to fight and is left reeling from the attack. A 'fight or flight' response is triggered in the surprised and unprepared victim, resulting in hurt, pain and suffering. If the 'victim' then falls into the trap of being triggered, what began as an expression of an opinion turns into an all-out 'take no prisoners' battle! The atmosphere becomes poisoned, while the psychological damage caused to both parties can end up being intense.

We are all too familiar with this scenario. It is regrettably often enacted on TV and in movies, making it seem almost normal, or even acceptable, which it most certainly is not. Worse still, when it is viewed as commonplace and enacted in the home, the impact on children can be devastating. They will not only suffer the wounds, often blaming themselves for the altercation with their parents, but also carry its memory into their subconscious. They end up repeating the same behaviour themselves.

Toxicity travels easily and is very contagious. Witness the behaviour of children of toxic parents who see their parents as role-models and assume that their behaviour is the right one to exhibit. Such children need help and support, often professional help. They have to be able to understand what they are experiencing and their associated feelings, how they have arisen and how to handle them before they become ingrained and detrimental to their future prospects. This is where the right kind of role-models are so badly needed.

Toxicity, like ego, works in very subtle and insidious ways, creeping into relationships stealthily yet relentlessly. It often begins with an apparent plea for help, a plaintive 'poor me' cry of help to elicit sympathy. This is particularly attractive to the kinder, empathetic, sensitive and vulnerable person. They are also seeking to be valued and loved. They crave love and affection and present a perfect target.

In many respects, this type of toxicity is even more dangerous. It develops more surreptitiously, over a longer time scale, and is more difficult to detect. And when it is at last perceived, it is too late. The poison has been activated and is that much harder to remove. The toxic person, often outwardly charming and approachable, will often bombard the victim with messages and texts, weekly flowers and expressions of affection and love, which completely takes in the willing, naïve and adoring victim. This more deceitful toxicity can be much harder to recognize because it is so covert, and, thus, much more difficult to handle once exposed.

By the time the truth has emerged, which it always will, the victim is fully ensnared and emotionally engaged. The victim is left feeling abandoned, alternatively outraged then guilty. Often they blame themselves in the process and wonder how what seemed such a beautiful relationships could have fallen apart so quickly.

Worse still the victim often tries to salvage the situation by accepting the abuse and pandering to the needs of the perpetrator in a desperate hope that they will change. They will not. People do not change because of the entreaties or actions of others. They only change when they themselves see the light and realize the importance of changing.

However overtly or subtly toxicity manifests itself, we need to recognize it in all its forms. We have to be very aware when we are in its presence if we are to succeed in managing and controlling its effects. Recognising toxicity before it becomes a problem for us is essential and saves much subsequent heartache.

In order to recognize toxicity, we all possess a vital tool: our instincts. We need to hone and trust them because they can be very helpful in distinguishing between genuine care and affection and false charm. Our instincts are a reflection of the emotions, vibrations and energy we feel. They are sometimes more useful as a guide than our intellect, our conscious reasoning, which has all kinds of other logical overlays and often fools itself into seeing the most desired outcome, not necessarily the most realistic one. Once committed, the conscious mind tries desperately to find evidence to support its belief and will clutch at any straw.

Whereas our body, if listened to carefully, will always respond to negatively charged vibrations and will sense this dark energy. The body never lies. The conscious mind may not see the danger and will try to gloss over it and find excuses and 'logical' explanations. When we are in the presence of toxicity, we will feel certain negative vibrations, emotions and physical responses. We should heed them, however difficult and disappointing that may be! Toxicity is like quicksand. It may look innocuous but is in reality a dreadful trap.

As we begin to train our instincts, it is very helpful to be able to recognize some of the more common 'discomforts' and warning signals. To aid with this, we have assembled a list of feelings to be aware of in your body. It is not exhaustive, but does provide guidance on what to be aware of.

If you sense any of the following, it is likely to be a signal that you are in the presence of toxicity. If so, be very awake and vigilant. *Caveat qui sentit!* Beware he or she who feels!

1. We feel a negative energy whenever the person is around; others feel the same way.
2. We find it hard to relax in their presence. We feel there's something not right.
3. We fear or dread any interaction with them, (especially if this means raising potentially contentious issues) for fear of their erratic and often deeply negative reaction.
4. We dare not make any criticism, however benign and diplomatically delivered, for fear of their response.

5. We often have the feeling we are being manipulated and controlled.
6. We only feel wanted and appreciated when the person needs us.
7. We are not given the full picture, feel lied to or kept in the dark. There is something secretive about the other person's behaviour as though they do not trust us.
8. Promises made are not always kept.
9. We often feel blamed, even for minor issues.
10. We feel the other person rejects personal responsibility for mishaps they have created and claims they are the one to have been let down, wronged or not listened to.
11. We feel the other party does not accept they might be wrong. They adopt the position of 'I told you so,' even though they never did anything to resolve the problem or grasp the opportunity at the time.
12. They rarely apologize.
13. After any interaction, we end up feeling bad.
14. We feel we are constantly 'giving' and pleasing with little or no positive response or reciprocity.
15. We feel our efforts go unnoticed and unacknowledged, and we are rarely thanked or recognized.
16. The relationship is asymmetric. There is an unequal contribution to the partnership.
17. We feel that whatever we try to do never seems to be enough and does not satisfy, please or impress, however hard we try.

18. We feel we are constantly 'walking on eggshells'. It is difficult to relax and be oneself.
19. We feel exhausted rather than energised.
20. We feel caught in an endless struggle of trying to help, care, fix and rescue but to little avail.
21. We feel unheard and that every helpful and constructive suggestion we make is rebuffed.
22. We find it hard to uphold our own values and compromise them to keep the peace.
23. We feel belittled.
24. We sometimes give up emotionally and feel we have to withdraw to maintain our sanity.
25. There is no laughter, no fun, too much negativity. Humour seems to be absent.
26. Everything is all much too serious.

3

Why and How Does Toxicity Occur?

Underlying psychological causes of toxicity

The all-important role of ego

A common trait of toxic people is that they are almost entirely controlled by their ego. By 'ego' we mean a false sense of self. They have created an image of themselves to which they have become attached and which they will protect at all cost. This image is excessively self-serving. It allows them to believe that they are better, more worthy and more deserving than anyone else. They demonstrate this in any and all interactions—whatever the consequences for others. This outward show of bravado, however, hides very low self-esteem and self-confidence, which is compounded by poor or little self-awareness.

They are so trapped in this unconscious self-absorbed state and illusory belief, that their ego, and the thoughts, emotions and actions emanating from it, has completely taken over. It is, in effect, controlling them. In this respect they are truly 'out of control'. When this is combined with a lack of empathy, a general unwillingness to change and complete indifference to the damaging and hurtful impact they have on others, we are in the presence of evil.

Toxicity = evil = uncontrolled ego = the dark shadow of repressed emotions.

The fact is that their actions are the product of their warped, conditioned thinking, which leads them to believe that they are somehow different, more special and justifiably 'separate' from everyone else. They feel superior to those around them. They gossip negatively even about (especially about!) their friends and are invariably right and others wrong.

There always seems to be drama in their life and they seem to attract and be surrounded by it. They are quick to blame, complain and criticize others and bemoan their bad fortune (indicating a 'dysfunctional personality disorder'). They prefer to blame their problems on others, their inherited genes, the government, even their own 'kind' nature!

Depending on their level of toxicity they may, on occasion, present a deeply remorseful side after a major bout of toxic, even violent, behaviour (which likely indicates a 'manic personality disorder'). But do not be fooled! This remorseful state is likely to be short-lived and as soon as they are forgiven, 'normal' (toxic) behaviour will resume.

Because they are generally unaware of how their ego is controlling them and lack the ability to create a space for objective self-reflection, they are on autopilot. It is difficult for anyone, however well-meaning, to change them. Ego relishes and depends for its survival on conflict. Ego enjoys soliciting as much reaction as possible, since this justifies and validates its existence. Receiving any reactive attention allows their ego to feel vindicated and its identity sustained and strengthened. Without conflict ego dies, and since it is ego that is driving the toxic process, conflict must happen.

All aggressive behaviour betrays deep insecurities, an absence of self-awareness, self-confidence and low self-esteem. All of which the ego attempts to cover up with outward shows of confidence. At some time in the past, toxic people were deeply hurt and wounded. It could be the recent past, but more commonly the hurt was in the distant past, probably childhood, and has been repetitively reinforced ever since.

This hurt could be from having been ignored, unloved, criticised, dismissed, belittled, bullied and/or abused. Sometimes it is the other extreme, they were spoiled, pampered and allowed to get their own way for the sake of peace. They may have been allowed (sometimes even encouraged) to act disrespectfully, unkindly and vengefully towards others—mimicking parental behaviour. These traits have then been carried forward into school, clubs, further education, the workplace and relationships, where they have continued to be 'refined'.

Very regrettably, it is not considered part of the education process to deal with such matters in anything other than a cursory manner. As studies have shown, the reason why some toxic pupils obtain satisfactory exam results and are hurried through to the next level is because their current teacher wishes to get them out of their class as soon as possible. Unable to obtain proper help for managing such students, teachers are left with little choice other than to take the easy way out for the sake of the other children and their own sanity.

The fact is that toxic people have never addressed, wanted to address or known how to come to terms with their trauma. It has become a dark shadow that follows them everywhere. And it will continue to do so until it is treated properly, most likely by a professional (such as a behavioural psychologist, psychiatrist or hypnotherapist).

As Carl Jung said in *Aion*:

> The psychological rule says that when an inner situation is not made conscious, it happens outside as fate.

And elaborated on in *On the Psychology of the Unconscious*:

> It is a frightening thought that man has a shadow side to him, consisting not just of little weaknesses and foibles, but of a positively demonic dynamism. The individual seldom knows anything of this; to him, as an individual, it is incredible that he should in any circumstances go beyond himself. But let these harmless creatures form a mass, and there emerges a raging monster.

Or as Jung's mentor, Sigmund Freud, put it in his *Introductory Lectures on Psycho-Analysis*:

> Unexpressed emotions will never die. They are buried alive and will come forth later in uglier ways.

Unexpressed emotions and untreated traumas will have been experienced at an early age. These can have included vicious internal family conflicts, harsh divorces, insensitive, unkind or violent parents. Negative behaviour surrounded the now toxic individual at an impressionable, formative and sensitive age. They have been conditioned to consider this behaviour normal. It has left painful scars that have not been faced, let alone acknowledged, accepted or cleansed. Nor has anyone helped them in this area.

They have not examined why they behave in this toxic manner. They have never forgiven those who wounded them because they do not know how to or have any inkling as to the psychological necessity of doing so.

As a consequence, they exhibit the same negative behaviours as those who first hurt them: bully, manipulator, deceiver, liar, ultra-perfectionist, martyr, tyrant, victim, critic. This pattern of behaviour becomes repetitive and compulsive and is responsible for most antisocial, psychopathic and criminal behaviours.

The absence of empathy or self-awareness and its impact

Highly toxic people have little or no empathy or self-awareness. This inability to put themselves in other people's shoes or to respect the feelings of others allows them to pursue any action, however destructive, to satisfy their own needs or wants. Other people's feelings and sensitivities just do not matter and are irrelevant to their thinking.

Over the centuries, this dangerous concept of justification has given rise to prejudices of all kinds, against anyone with whom the toxic person or collective disagrees. As far as toxic people are concerned others are simply there to meet their needs and do their bidding. It is the ultimate selfishness. Their level of consciousness is so low as to be described as 'unconscious'.

Highly judgmental, toxic people frequently attach labels to people. This is another of ego's tricks to make itself different and superior while putting others down. Labelling people in this way condemns them to narrow boxes, which has the intended effect of belittling, devaluing and dehumanizing. Dehumanizing makes it easier and seemingly more justifiable to abuse the victims of this dehumanisation. There is no risk of the need for sympathy or remorse. Since the victims are projected as no longer human, they automatically become less worthy of respect.

With this warped thinking, it is easy to see how compassion for others is replaced by disrespect, disdain and hate. Ego needs to blame and to find scapegoats and toxic people are highly skilled at finding others to take responsibility for their own failings.

Many of the world's greatest tragedies have resulted from this type of toxic thinking—between both individuals and nations. No wars have ever been fought, or genocides ever committed, by people who did not believe themselves to be decent human beings or were not convinced that 'right' and 'justice' were on their side. Think of the priests involved in the Spanish Inquisition, employing torture and execution in the name of God against those they saw as 'heretics'.

This strategy of labelling 'others' is designed to coerce and control through brutality and fear. It has been used through history by those who share the same psychotically and pathologically toxic characteristics. Alas, it continues to be used today. One only has to read the news to be aware of the toxicity of dictatorial leaders. They are more concerned with their own image, wealth, power and survival than the people they are supposed to nurture, protect and inspire.

The 'aura' that toxicity transmits is contagiously negative. A toxic person can depress and destabilize the atmosphere and harmony of any group, meeting or conversation very rapidly. They can make the happy unhappy in an instant. They are rarely upbeat about life and seem to find a way of making even positive news seem negative.

Toxic people are themselves often highly strung, thin-skinned and acutely sensitive to perceived slights and critical comments, which they take personally. Rather than considering constructive criticism as an opportunity to learn and change, they hate any form of criticism and often react violently to any suggestion regarding their own behaviour or its negative effect on others.

Caught in a spiral of negativity, they show scant appreciation for the wonders of life. They find it difficult to praise or thank others or feel genuine gratitude for help or kindness. They rarely feel a sense of awe and amazement about anything or show genuine excitement or enthusiasm. Not surprisingly, being in constant conflict with themselves, they suffer from high levels of anxiety and generate destructive levels of stress for those around them.

Many studies have shown the very detrimental damage to the body caused by high levels of cortisol as a consequence of anxiety and stress. In addition to the damage caused to the physical and psychological self, the individual and collective performance and harmony of the group can also be severely affected.

An arena where group harmony and performance are particularly badly affected by toxicity and its resultant stress is the workplace. We shall explore this in detail in the next chapter.

4

Workplace Toxicity

Toxic bosses, toxic peers

It is normal for there to be a certain level of stress in the workplace, given the high-pressure demands on organizations and their people and the justifiable ambitions of companies. In such circumstances, stress can be a valuable contributor to dynamism, creativity and energy. This is called *eustress.*

It is, however, the unnecessary and often unexpected stress caused by toxic people that creates the greatest harm and dysfunctionality. It can destroy the entire harmony of the organization. Toxic people in the workplace show up in various forms, all of which need to be exposed and understood.

Although toxic workplace characters come in all shapes and sizes, we've distilled them into five types of 'bosses' and five 'peers'. There is, naturally, some crossover behaviour, however, by categorizing the types it will help you recognize them easily.

Toxic bosses

a) The Ruthless Hyper-Ambitious/Narcissistic Dictator

Such bosses are only interested in their image, careers and themselves. They will do practically anything to achieve success (in the form of promotion, wealth or recognition) even if this means riding roughshod over employees and colleagues. They have no empathy whatsoever and do not care about people. They only care about themselves.

The idea that a company might have an ethos or a purpose is entirely irrelevant to them, unless it benefits their image and career. If it does not serve them directly, they have no time to waste on such extravagances.

They do have a lot of energy , but apply it to their driving ambition. Because they are able to focus this energy single-mindedly on themselves, they will achieve initial results. But it will be at a heavy price, ultimately to themselves, but most immediately for their environment. They leave a trail of disappointed, hurt and demotivated employees.

As long as people are of use to them, they will tolerate them, even encourage them and give the impression that they support them. But as soon as anyone objects to their demands or, worse still, disagrees with them, they will become angry, vengeful and ruthless and ignore the person from then on. They expect undying loyalty, lots of sacrifices and total commitment, but will not repay that loyalty with their own. They will not give credit where it is due and will move on to their next assignment without a second thought. Often, they leave behind a mass of problems for their successor.

b) The Overpromoted

Many bosses, having managed to obtain their promotion, find it very hard to rise to the next level of leadership. This is the Peter principle in action: people get promoted to their 'level of incompetence' and they cannot move on. They seek comfort and the illusion of success by continuing to do their previous job in their new role. This displacement activity not only results in them not doing their own job, which is serious enough, but it also stops their successor doing theirs! This behaviour is toxic for both their successor and the entire team.

c) The Micromanager

Micromanagers suffer from a form of OCD. Their profound absence of self-confidence, in themselves and projected on to their employees and peers, inevitably leads to the habit of over monitoring and double checking everything. They have the false belief that this display of duplicate energy will result in better performance. As in the case of the overpromoted, this displacement activity is highly irritating. It puts off competent and imaginative initiative takers and is highly wasteful in time and energy. This toxic behaviour significantly reduces effectiveness—not to mention team cohesion!

d) The Lazy Boss

Laziness is toxic. Lazy bosses may give the impression of being good delegators and 'hands off', but this is highly misleading. Their real skill lies in catching up frantically at the last moment and, above all, winging it. They are clearly adept at impressing, not to say hoodwinking their own bosses (that's, after all, how they attained their position) and may well be charmingly charismatic. They have achieved their position by doing as little as possible (not reading background papers, not listening to advice, not initiating meetings) and relying on the hard work of their employees. Only when the time comes to deliver results will they be stirred into action. At that point, they become highly anxious and flustered from not being in control of their material. They flap about in nervous agitation, firing questions indiscriminately and requesting information (most of which has already been provided, but they have not bothered to read) to catch up and alleviate their anxiety. They will cheerfully take credit for any successes, since this relieves them of any feelings of guilt concerning their laziness. For similar reasons, they will not properly recognize the work of others.

e) The Disrespectful Boss

Disrespectful bosses are highly toxic to any organisation. Their lack of respect can take a number of forms: ignoring colleagues and employees alike; refusing to discuss matters that require others' inputs; dismissing the views of others; seeking to take over decision-making; being aggressive and rude; and acting through fear and intimidation. People are only important to them insofar as they can assist them in the pursuit of their own objectives and needs. The lack of recognition of the feelings of others signals a lack of humanness generally. It is very disruptive to the individuals and teams of any organisation. Such bosses are prone to belittle, bully, harass or worse. Their behaviour goes against the principles and values of any decent company and will cause much disquiet.

Toxic peers

a) Ruthless, Ambitious, Competitive

These colleagues have only one purpose in life: to make it to the highest position possible as quickly as possible. They will use practically any means to do so and will be particularly adept at 'managing upwards', that is, being as helpful and accommodating as possible to their bosses to curry favour. Their obsequiousness will grate with their peers but may well be appreciated by the gullible boss. They will use any means necessary to obtain promotion and have no qualms about lying or cheating to get there. They do not take responsibility for their actions—especially mishaps, where they will look for scapegoats. They view colleagues and anyone below them as competitors and consider it totally appropriate to damage others if it serves them.

b) Credit Takers

Credit takers have many similar characteristics and ambitions to the first category, but are specialists at finding ways to take the credit due to others. They behave ostensibly as friends but will not hesitate to betray a trust or steal an idea if it enables them to be seen in a better light by the boss. They appear to be good team members but will happily belittle the contribution others have made, or, when possible, simply omit to mention them.

c) Intimidators

Intimidators again share similar objectives to the first two categories, but have a different modus operandi. They use their connections inside the company to impress and intimidate peers and colleagues, as well as people below them. They can be jovial and enthusiastic and will come over as the heart and soul of the party, but their intention is to take over the group. They achieve this with a mixture of intimidation and fear—behaviour that will stimulate conflict and toxicity.

d) Free Riders

These are the employee equivalents of the lazy boss. They are very skilled at doing as little as possible. They even deliberately do tasks poorly, so someone else has to help complete them. They do not like to make any special efforts and will resist any requests for voluntary work or spending additional hours. They plead either a lack of time (because they claim to be working on something else of greater importance) or a lack of requisite knowledge. They do not pull their weight and, again, create a toxic, discordant and quarrelsome environment.

e) Gossipers/Gaslighters

This group lack confidence and feel inadequate, they compensate by disrupting and unbalancing others, which, perversely, makes them feel superior. To further their image of themselves and damage that of others, gossipers will 'tell tales out of school', even if this means betraying a confidence. They use any information, even if untrue or only partly true, to project their own anxieties and insecurities on to others. Weaker, more naïve colleagues risk being 'gaslighted' through their web of lies. Gossipers and gaslighters are very toxic to the cohesion of any team. Their bullying—because that is what it is—is particularly injurious to the new entrant or the more introverted and reserved, who make tempting targets.

Unfortunately, while there are well-meaning, balanced and hardworking bosses and peers, toxicity is all-pervasive in the workplace. It only takes one bad apple to cause rotting in the orchard. That is why it is critical for individuals and corporations to learn how to handle toxicity. The toxicity they themselves are responsible for and the toxicity that arises from others.

Corporates need, therefore, to teach all employees to recognize, manage and eradicate toxicity whenever it arises. This will reduce stress, improve physical and psychological wellbeing and encourage harmonious working practices. The results will create and stimulate an environment in which all can contribute fully, effectively and happily.

5

The Importance of Understanding Our Own Toxicity

We all have the capacity to be toxic!

To start understanding toxicity and then mastering the techniques for managing it, it is critical for us to be very mindful of our own capacity for toxicity. In any toxic situation, there have to be at least two people. Everyone shares responsibility for the outcome.

The first step to grasping our own toxicity is to see that some interactions seem toxic purely because of the way we ourselves choose to view them. It may well be that there is no inherent toxicity. Rather the toxicity occurs as a consequence of our own sensitivity and our perception of the person or situation.

This sensitivity could be triggered by someone's tone of voice, body language, pace of delivery, attitude or facial expression. We need to be able to consciously separate what is truly toxic from our personal and individual reaction to situations that happen to cause *us* discomfort, but which have no malice behind them. We often react to our own sensitivities rather than appreciating the true nature of the event.

As Epictetus said in the *Enchiridion*:

> Men are disturbed not by things, but by the views which they take of things.

In such cases, the resolution is in our own hands, and we need to take active responsibility.

In the words of Marcus Aurelius:

> If you are distressed by anything external, the pain is not due to the thing itself, but to your estimate of it; and this you have the power to revoke at any moment.

Or as Shunryu Suzuki says:

> Nothing outside yourself can cause you any trouble. You yourself make the waves in your mind. If you leave your mind as it is, it will become calm.
>
> —*Zen Mind, Beginner's Mind*

In these cases, the opportunity to avoid or remedy what seems to be a toxic situation lies with us rather than the other person. It is often we ourselves who are feeling overlooked, belittled, ignored or unloved. Our sensitivity is the cause of the 'toxicity'.

Another cause of 'toxic' situations that are not due to another person's toxicity is when we are feeling a little off colour. As a consequence, we are the ones choosing to withdraw, become grumpy or overly aggressive, needy or petulant. This kind of situation has nothing to do with the supposed toxicity of the other person but rather with our own ego and toxicity.

From the above examples, it should be clear that when faced with a person who causes us discomfort, rather than immediately blaming them it is vital that we look inside ourselves *first*.

For this, we need to have the emotional intelligence (EQ) to understand our own feelings. We have to be aware of our behaviours and how we tend to react under different circumstances. It is our responsibility to have the humility and courage to understand better who we are.

This takes proper, quiet time to reflect carefully and is what is meant by self-awareness. (A study by Cornell School of Industrial and Labor relations (2010) found self-awareness to be the strongest predictor of overall success of leaders, which is totally understandable in this context.) It is a critical first step and is what Aristotle talks about when he writes:

Knowing yourself is the beginning of all wisdom.

Self-awareness is the key to defusing many otherwise destructive toxic situations and rendering them harmless before they become problematic. We all have the capacity to be toxic ourselves and to act in an unconsciously disagreeable manner at times. Our toxicity can be triggered by an external stimulus or internally by our own 'self-worth' or ego.

Some of us are very sensitive to the mood and feelings of friends and colleagues, others less so. Some of us are very conscious of the effect we have on others, of the impact of our words, body language and behaviour on those around us and others less so. Some of us are slow to anger while others take offence more easily. Some of us feel empathy and deep compassion for others, while others are more dispassionate and disengaged. The fact is that we are, thankfully, all different.

However different our personalities, we do all have egos! (We are using 'ego' in the sense that we are all conditioned to be unrealistic about who we are and we believe this illusionary image of ourselves.) As a result, we all have the capacity to be triggered into toxicity. And we have all been toxic at some time or another.

Toxicity is part of the human condition and the 'duality' of human existence. Duality means that everything automatically has its opposite. That is the universal law of polarity. North implies south. Hot implies cold. Up implies down. Good implies bad. Life implies death. You cannot have one without the other.

Therefore, toxicity implies empathy and kindness. We would not know what toxicity is unless we also knew what empathy was. Toxicity and empathy may be very different in nature, but they are implicitly inseparable.

This is an important point. We need to understand that we cannot deny, let alone eliminate, toxicity any more than we can deny or eliminate ego. The two are inextricably linked. This means, in our own case, that rather than denying the existence of toxicity within us, we must learn to be aware of its presence. We need to notice when it appears, observe it and how it operates. By learning to recognize its causes and symptoms, we can master and manage them.

The best way to deal with the toxicity of others is to have first observed deeply, been very awake to and have mastered our own toxicity. When we know and understand our own 'darkness', we are much better equipped to understand the darkness of others, as Jung observed.

> Anybody whose calling it is to guide souls should have his own soul guided first, so that he knows what it means to deal with the human soul.
>
> Knowing your own darkness is the best method for dealing with the darknesses of other people.
>
> —Carl Jung, letter to Kendig B. Cully

We will discuss *darkness* and the *shadow* in depth in question vi) of chapter 7. However, the first step in developing self-awareness is to understand the important difference between *observing* and *judging*.

Observing means being objectively aware or conscious. Of what? Our strengths and weaknesses. After observing, we can then choose to do something about them—or not. This is opposed to judging, which immediately adds a label and pigeonholes the characteristic. This closes down the opportunity for beneficial change. It then becomes much harder to accept the 'what is' of the trait and be open and constructive about what to do about it.

We should observe carefully who we are, how we think and react to different stimuli, how what we do or say affects others and what matters to us. This process allows us gradually to learn about ourselves in a dispassionate and calm way. We learn that we are as we are. And that's fine. We can now decide to do whatever we want. We have total freedom of choice. We can be who we want to be. That is our discipline and that is our power. And it is immense. But we have to accept ourselves first.

When we learn to accept ourselves without judgment, we have created the circumstances to also learn to accept others for who they are—without judgement—which builds a solid foundation for more harmonious relationships. In this way, we are learning to become detached from and not react to—not take personally—the ego of others.

> When you realize it's not personal, there is no longer a compulsion to react as if it were. By not reacting to the ego, you will often be able to bring out the sanity in others, which is the unconditioned consciousness as opposed to the conditioned. At times you may have to take practical steps to protect yourself from deeply unconscious people. This you can do without making them into enemies. Your greatest protection, however, is being conscious.
>
> —Eckhart Tolle, *A New Earth*

To appreciate our own susceptibilities in all humility is an essential precondition to learning to manage toxicity. No mortal being is 'perfect'—in the sense of having no faults (thank goodness!)—we all have our weaknesses, as well as our strengths. That is what makes us human. In learning how to deal with the toxicity of others, we have to learn to recognize and deal with our own.

This is not a natural process but rather one that has to be examined and learned. There is no room for complacency or ego. We cannot conceitedly assume that we are never toxic ourselves. Nor that this is always someone else's issue. No one is immune from being toxic themselves—even if it's only occasionally. And in all relationships, it takes two to tango.

It is thus incumbent on us to take time to observe our own behaviours, which means taking note of what triggers us and why.

We have to be witness to the workings of our ego and see how the false sense of our own importance leads us to think and act destructively. While it is always valuable to recognize this in hindsight and feel remorse, it is far wiser to be pre-warned and pre-armed and avoid the conflict, damage and pain in the first place.

Understanding our reactions and learning to manage them is critical if we are to have any chance of dealing effectively with the considerable problems and suffering posed by toxicity. We need to know who we are and be comfortable with and accept ourselves—faults and all. With this understanding, nothing can unwittingly shake us or send us off course.

Reflecting on and understanding our own mind is a key to managing toxicity.

> Nothing in the world can bother you as much as your own mind, I tell you. In fact, others seem to be bothering you, but it is not others, it is your own mind.
>
> —Sri Sri Ravi Shankar

6

Managing Our Own Toxicity

To change your life outside, first you have to change inside

Having taken time to observe our own thinking and be the witness of who we really are, we can then take active steps to manage our own toxicity. The benefits of this cannot be overestimated. The learning we obtain from this process will not only provide us with a deeper self-awareness and understanding of our toxicity, but also provide us with suitable tools to change ourselves, while enhancing our self-confidence in using them appropriately.

> One can only face in others what one can face in oneself.
>
> —James Baldwin,
> *Nobody Knows My Name*

We should never expect others to change (or seek to change them ourselves) because this does not work. But we can change ourselves and our perceptions of life, other people and events. In so doing, we can learn to handle difficult people and situations in a completely different way—less stressful and more effective and compassionate. It makes sense because being in toxic situations is exhausting to the central nervous system and takes up huge amounts of psychic energy that would be better deployed on more productive and constructive matters.

That changing ourselves first is of critical importance was recognized many years ago. This wisdom was encapsulated in one of the Delphic maxims (inscribed in the forecourt of the Temple of Apollo at Delphi): *Gnothi seauton,* or Know thyself. And many philosophers and sages have expressed this same truth:

> Knowing others is intelligence, knowing yourself is true wisdom.
>
> —Lao Tzu, Tao Te Ching

> The unexamined life is not worth living.
>
> —Socrates

> He knows the universe and does not know himself.
>
> —Jean De La Fontaine, *Fables*

In recent times, the Wachowskis reflected this truth in their film *The Matrix. Temet nosce* ('Know thyself' in Latin) is inscribed over the Oracle's door.

Understanding and then changing our life from the inside is a precondition for changing life outside. In other words, if we want to manage toxicity outside, we have to learn to manage it inside ourselves first.

> In order to change your life outside, you must first change inside.
>
> —Louise Hay

One of my secrets for attracting … abundance into my life has been an internal axiom that … goes like this: *Change the way you look at things and the things you look at change.…* The truth of this little maxim is actually found in the field of quantum physics … It turns out that at the tiniest subatomic level, the actual act of observing a particle changes the particle. The way we observe these infinitely small building blocks of life is a determining factor in what they ultimately become.… Changing the way you look at things is an extremely powerful tool. Start by examining how you look at things.

—Wayne Dyer, 'Success Secrets'

The fountain of content must spring up in the mind, and he who hath so little knowledge of human nature as to seek happiness by changing anything but his own disposition, will waste his life in fruitless efforts and multiply the grief he proposes to remove.

—Samuel Johnson

The chief task in life is this: to identify and separate matters so that I can say clearly to myself which are externals not under my control, and which have to do with the choices I actually control. Where then do I look for good and evil? Not to uncontrollable externals, but within myself to the choices that are my own.

—Epictetus, *Discourses*

Work on yourself, find the issues within and work on them. Once you have mastered them, then you're ready. We are creatures of habit, so learn what habits are causing the issues and work on developing new ones. 20% of the things you're doing is causing 80% of the problems. Change the 20% and you see a massive difference in your life.

—Jon Covey

7

What Issues Within Should We Observe and Change?

Questions that help us identify our own toxicity

Everything that applies to toxic people and indicates the presence of toxicity (which we indicated in the list at the end of chapter 2) can also apply to us.

The rest of this chapter consists of a series of powerful questions that can help you identify your own toxicity and its causes. These are complemented with relevant guidance on how to manage that toxicity. It can also be very helpful to solicit constructive feedback in this process. (For guidance on feedback, see question vi) below, especially part f).)

Learning to manage our own toxicity gives us powerful insights into managing toxic people and toxic situations. By understanding our own capacity for toxicity and learning to deal with it, we create our own practice laboratory.

This process allows us to be more compassionate about the toxicity of others. It does not mean we accept toxic behaviour, but our empathetic knowledge will help us identify and manage it that much better.

Being aware of our own toxicity. Questions to ask and consider carefully

i) Are we better listeners or talkers?

To manage a toxic situation, we need to understand first and be understood second. This requires a high level of active listening. Showing a sincere desire to understand the toxic person or situation, as well as listening for the real cause of the problem, is critical to finding a resolution.

If we prefer to talk first and seek to be understood before understanding the real problem, we are likely to trigger an adverse reaction, or make a bad situation worse. People who are too quick to express themselves risk being insensitive and overbearing, leaving others behind, ignored and hurt. Such behaviour can easily become toxic.

Observing how often we speak first and then learning to positively hold back and let others speak first is a useful exercise. This is easier said than done. It is habit changing and requires several months of practice before it becomes second nature. But the effort will be immensely rewarding and rewarded.

Being a good, active listener is an essential quality for receiving helpful feedback. It is also vital in receiving and interpreting key signals from toxic people. We are then better able to respond and defuse as necessary.

We can also practise our listening skills during quiet times or meditation. Simply listen to all the sounds around us, without judgment or labelling. When we listen to music, we can learn to listen to the gaps between the sounds and hear that music is not continuous but a rapid alternation of sound and silence.

ii) Do we think first and react second or the other way around?

This question follows on from the first, but addresses our emotional reactions and what we say and hear rather than our intellect. When anything is said or done (or simply when we read or watch something) it is normal for us to have an internal reaction that is felt in our body. The actual location of that feeling (heart, stomach/guts, head, shoulders) is also important and tells us which emotion is being affected (love, fear, anxiety, stress). If what is said or seen contradicts what we believe or violates our values (or even our hopes and expectations), we may experience an intense bodily reaction. There is nothing wrong with any of that: it shows we are sensitive and vulnerable human beings.

But when we react indiscriminately—letting people know immediately and exactly how we feel, without first considering the circumstance or the audience—it can quickly lead to toxicity. People who react too quickly, without having taken time to reflect, will be inherently toxic and will easily alienate friends and colleagues. Who wants to be with someone who always says exactly what they feel, irrespective of whether it offends or hurts others?

Reacting is *re*-acting, that is, acting again. This means to experience the same emotional reaction over and over again. Our re-actions have a repetitive nature and have become automatic. Moreover, we believe that the cause of our emotional reaction is the action or behaviour of another. We believe we have been triggered by something someone has done *to us*.

That is not the case. For example, if we are 'cut up' on the motorway or ignored in a queue, no one has actually done anything *to us*. It is *our* perception of what has happened that has caused us to be triggered.

The true cause of our reaction—and why we keep repeating it over again—lies somewhere in our conditioned past. Every time the same circumstances occur, we re-act accordingly—like a robot. It is easiest to put the blame for our discomfort on another. But this other is not the cause, just a messenger, reminding us that we have unresolved issues, which we still have to address. And until we do that, we will continue to re-act. Our toxic behaviour is the *effect* of our unmanaged conditioned past. How to deal with this conditioning is the subject of much of *Toxicum*, but is especially covered in question vi) of this chapter.

Even without fully addressing our conditioned past, we can reduce our capacity to react toxically to triggers. Carefully observing our feelings and disciplining ourselves to pause and take two or three breaths before reacting will greatly help us. This requires a level of personal discipline and the establishment of a new and healthier habit. In order to create new habits, we need to reflect consciously during periods of quiet contemplation or meditation and then practise whenever the occasion arises. Instead of blasting the messenger, we should welcome the message. Embrace the opportunity to show that you can consciously observe and deal with the issues as they present themselves.

The results of this discipline and exercise are well worth the effort.

iii) Are we aware of our ego? Can we observe it? Can we let it go when we need to?

We all have an ego. We feel an identity. As we grow up, we come to understand that characteristics are attributed to us. Some of them are inherent in our birth situation—race, physical aspects and social situation. Others are created by our parents, their perspective on life, their behaviour towards us, their expectations. And some we gradually acquire through experience, education, sports, the workplace, the reactions of others, as well as all our own reactions to life. As a result, we form a view of who we think we are. That is ego.

However, ego is an illusion and a delusion. It is not real. It is just a thought, a figment of our imagination that we believe to be real and then take seriously. When we try to describe who we are, we respond most frequently by saying our name and then what we have done, our status, our role in society. We then go on to expand on our achievements, accolades and acquisitions. We do not describe who we really are, but what we have done and who we would like to believe we are. This is ego.

It is not the truth. Our personality is an act. The word comes from 'persona', meaning a mask. Ego is a mask—or rather a series of masks—that we wear to demonstrate who we would like to be, or who we think others expect us to be. It is a role we fool ourselves into playing as if it were real. It is pure make-believe—designed to impress, not to inform.

Ego tells lies without qualm—to its host (of which it is an inescapable part) and to anyone around. It is the ultimate magician and trickster making the unreal seem real, falsehoods appear true. Moreover, it can be hard to detect and decipher, especially in ourselves. As human beings, we have an extraordinary predilection for self-delusion. However, make no mistake:

> *Ego—this unexamined, poorly understood, immensely powerful psychological phenomenon—is the prime source of all toxicity. It is the cause of the world's greatest tragedies. Unfettered, it will also destroy us.*

Sociopathic, psychopathic, narcissistic behaviour is highly toxic primarily because the ego is literally out of control. Jesus made this clear when he said: 'Forgive them, for they know not what they do.' The pharisees demanding Jesus' torture and crucifixion felt threatened. Or rather their egos felt threatened. Here was someone challenging their authority with great skill and popular success. Whether he might be right—showing a new way to live without toxicity, in peace and love—was totally irrelevant to them. Ego was threatened and ego must defend itself and win at any cost. The other must lose and be destroyed!

Understanding and observing our own ego requires deep reflection, self-awareness and maturity. We need the courage to face our fears and to be truthful. Being truthful and totally honest is very difficult but essential. Human beings have a remarkable capacity for self-deception—the work of ego again. Ego justifies and excuses actions known to be wrong. It elaborates and adds exaggerated ornamentation to stories that enhance our image, especially in the eyes of others. It falsifies information and tells blatant lies. If we are honest with ourselves, we know this to be true.

It does help us to cope with blunders and makes us temporarily feel better about ourselves. But it stops us from seeing the truth. And if we cannot see or accept the truth, which means accept who we really are, we are impoverished and diminished as human beings. Without truth or light, ego reigns supreme.

Observing ego is best done in silence, quietly, calmly, compassionately, truthfully. Learning how to walk away from distractions, taking time to reflect and learning to appreciate the calming effect of silence is essential and highly rewarding. We cannot think deeply when we're rushing around *doing* things. We can only truly reflect when we are *being*. Self-awareness is enhanced by quiet self-reflection.

Meditation is a wonderful way to calm the mind, reduce stress and anxiety and focus attention on who we really are and the role of ego in this process. It enables us to be more acutely aware of our thoughts, emotions and actions and how ego affects them.

As Eckhart Tolle wrote in *A New Earth*:

> Rather than being your thoughts and emotions, be the awareness behind them.

A thought echoed by Herman Melville:

> Silence is the general consecration of the universe...
> Silence is the only Voice of our God.

Or again, as expressed by psychotherapist and Buddhist practitioner Mark Epstein:

> Meditation is not a means of forgetting the ego; it is a method of using the ego to observe and tame its own manifestations.

iv) Do we know and understand our triggers?

When we start to feel riled, it is our body's physical reaction to a trigger. The trigger could be what someone says to us, how they say it (tone and loudness of voice, body language, facial expression), as well as the context in which they say it, such as whether other people are around.

Our emotional reaction is our own ego response. If someone says something to us that could be considered disagreeable, but we are in control of our ego, we will simply let it go and move on. 'Letting go' is acceptance and surrender. It is a wonderful quality to develop to take the venom out of toxicity.

However, when our ego is engaged and we feel a defensive reaction in our body and mind, then toxicity is stimulated. Ego will defend itself very actively when aroused. Its survival depends on winning the conflict. An unfettered ego will do practically anything, however toxic, to protect itself—even becoming violent if all else fails.

When we understand and recognize what constitutes a trigger for us, we anticipate our ego's reaction. It is essential, therefore, to be aware of these triggers. Make a regular note of them whenever they occur, ideally in a journal or diary, so you can absorb the lessons they offer at a later stage.

Clearly there are certain things that will tend to trigger most reasonable people: rudeness (and its physical signals); unwarranted abrupt orders or instructions; verbal or physical abuse; dismissive behaviour; arrogance; excessively negative or defeatist language; absence of recognition or gratitude; or comments seen as critical or insensitive. The list is extensive.

On closer inspection, however, you can observe that a trigger has engaged and enraged our ego, which then feels affronted and automatically fights back—unless overridden.

Examining how and why our ego reacts to different stimuli lies at the heart of knowing our triggers. And knowing our triggers is the key to managing them. Being pre-warned is to be pre-armed.

Understanding what triggers us will do much to help us understand, appreciate and manage the triggers of others with more compassion. What we see in others is, after all, a reflection of what we see in ourselves. It may be positive or negative, light or dark.

v) Can we recall what we were like growing up? How did we react to triggers then?

Many, if not all, our triggers are rooted in the past. How we reacted as a child to verbal or physical stimuli will be how we react now to similar situations. The triggers are likely to be the same—only modified by the passage of time and maturity.

Go back to your childhood and examine the feelings you had in the interactions with your parents. When they were supportive, what did they say and how did you feel and react? When they were critical, how did you feel and react? When they made suggestions about your physical appearance, your friends, what you wore, your hairstyle, your schoolwork or your behaviour, how did you feel and react? How did their reaction to your expressed hopes and ambitions (or lack of them), your degree of freedom, and your habits in general make you feel and react? Make a list of the things that happened that you can easily remember and note how you reacted. This is most likely how you react today to similar implied criticism or comments from family members, work colleagues or partners.

Go back to your schooldays and make a list of the comments of your teachers and how you reacted then. Make a list of the comments of your friends and peers, especially those with whom you did not enjoy the best of relationships.

And do the same as regards your reactions to the comments and actions of your peers, friends and colleagues today. What upsets you? What makes you withdraw? What makes you angry? What makes you become defensive? What gives you energy and enthusiasm?

What motivates you? What excites you? What fills you with joy? What fills you with dread? What are you most frightened of?

The examination of the causes of all our reactions provides valuable insights into our own psyche. We can extract many lessons, but this list will also prove extremely valuable as we move on to an examination of our dark side below in vi). These triggers are our unconscious reactions to our 'shadow'!

vi) Are we familiar with our 'dark' side. Have we confronted our 'shadow' and reconciled ourselves with it (integrated it to achieve some level of 'wholeness')?

Closely linked to an understanding of our ego, our triggers and responses is the difficult but essential examination of our shadow.

Our personal shadow, or alter ego, develops automatically from childhood and represents a little brother or sister to the developing ego from which it is inseparable. As we grow up, we learn to identify with personality characteristics we believe are the most helpful to us and which are reinforced by our family, peers, teachers and society. But, at the same time, we repress or bury those traits we are conditioned to think do not serve us and do not fit with our ego image of ourselves.

Those repressed traits become aspects of ourselves that we learn not to love and keep hidden away. Every part of our personality that we do not love is a hostage to fortune and will ultimately become hostile to us. Equally importantly, if we cannot love ourselves for who we are, we will find it impossible to truly love anyone else.

For example, if we are told that it is not 'manly' to be gentle or to cry, and these sentiments are reinforced by family and school, we learn to bury those 'feminine' qualities in the shadow of our subconscious mind. We then ignore or deny them. But they are still there with us—in our shadow. We cannot rid ourselves of them and they will resurface—most likely in a negative way—when we least expect it.

We are now conflicted within ourselves, and our psyche is effectively torn. Our natural tendency is towards gentleness, but our ego personality and the demands of our social environment require us to be 'tough', 'uncompromising' and 'strong'. The repressed feelings will come out in the form of inconsiderate behaviour and attitude—such as hatred, cruelty, bullying and anger—not least towards those people who exhibit the repressed qualities of gentleness and vulnerability. This can lead to psychopathology and criminal behaviour of the worst kind.

The same holds true for characteristics that are considered ideal such as hard-working, intelligent, polite and generous. We learn to adopt these as ego-promoting, self-serving traits, while confining to the shadow their opposites—namely laziness, stupidity, rudeness and selfishness. In this case, we then see our shadow in the 'nasty' behaviour of other people. We project the same negative characteristics in a futile attempt to distance ourselves from these distasteful behaviours and banish them from our own consciousness. We label others as stupid, lazy, self-centred and idiotic—creating ideal circumstances for rampant and prolonged toxicity.

All the feelings, emotions and behaviours that are rejected by ego are pushed into the shadow and constitute the dark side of our personality. They will reappear in one form or another until faced and brought to the light. Repression does not eliminate those qualities and characteristics we wish to hide or stop them from functioning as part of our psychic reactions. It simply removes them from our conscious ego-awareness. They continue as psychological complexes, but being removed from awareness means they are also removed from our control. Until control is regained, which is a deliberate and painful process, they are left to continue to affect us in an unchecked, disruptive and destructive manner. They reappear when we are in tough or difficult situations, in painful relationships or whenever toxicity surfaces.

Although the shadow is not all bad, as we shall see later, what makes it so dangerous and chaotic is precisely that it is repressed and hidden from our view. The light of our consciousness has disregarded it by design and out of fear. In the words of Carl Jung:

> [The unconscious] only becomes dangerous when our conscious attention to it is hopelessly wrong.

Discovering our shadow is no easy task because it has been deeply hidden away to 'protect' ourselves. Thus, we cannot see it ourselves directly, even though others can see it in our everyday behaviours and reactions.

However, this does not mean our shadow cannot be examined and positively addressed. We do so by developing our own individual consciousness and undertaking what is often referred to in spiritual and therapy circles as *shadow work*. This takes time, patience, considerable discipline and requires brutal, total honesty. It will be exceedingly painful at times, as we come to realize our own capacity for deeply negative and destructive thoughts, actions and behaviour. But this work is essential in developing our skills to tackle toxicity in all its forms. Toxicity is a loud manifestation of the shadow, as well as the ego, in all human beings.

The objective of shadow work is to understand and reconcile ourselves to our shadow in a compassionate but direct way, achieving what Carl Jung refers to as *individuation*. Individuation is when all the components of our psyche are integrated into a balanced whole. In this state, our personality achieves a state of *wholeness*. This enables us to transcend psychopathic and neurotic behaviour, overcome narcissism and confront toxicity in all its forms.

Shadow work implies 'owning' our shadow and developing a relationship with it that balances our conscious and unconscious sides. We comprehend our ego and its darker sibling and, ultimately, know who we are at the deepest level.

There are several ways in which we can learn to meet our shadow in everyday life:

a) Observing our humour

When we laugh at a risqué joke, at the person slipping on a banana skin or at the come-uppance of a pompous character, our laughter is an expression of our hidden, feared, inferiority-complexed shadow. We have been told that it is not appropriate to refer to a taboo body part or to laugh at the misfortune of others and have repressed these feelings. But when they are presented as comic or sudden happenings, our shadow side reveals itself in fits of laughter. It is the shadow that is laughing at the joke.

By observing our humour and what we consider to be funny, we get a view into our shadow. Taking a close look at what we think of as funny, or what others think of as funny, but we do not, will expose some interesting and relevant information about our shadow.

(A lack of a sense of humour probably indicates a very repressed shadow, according to the Jungian analyst and Episcopal priest John A Sanford. Since it is generally the shadow that laughs at the jokes, the absence of laughter indicates a highly repressed condition.)

b) Observing any excessively angry reaction to others

When we feel outrageously angry about someone else's faults or behaviours—either in a sudden eruption, or equally after allowing our mind to ruminate darkly—the shadow is expressing itself. This is the moment to explore calmly why this excess of anger is occurring and doing so before we push it away.

It is very easy to dismiss our 'shameful' reaction without examination, not least because confronting the shadow is a frightening, highly uncomfortable and even shocking process that can seriously dent our self-image of rationality and calm! Why might we be harbouring such horrible unkind, even violent thoughts? How could a relatively mundane situation trigger such deep feelings of envy, resentment, fear, hate or even suicidal thoughts? What is it that is causing this rage in us, this feeling of helpless inequity?

Excessively angry reactions should be observed and carefully considered since they are reflections of feelings that are repressed and that we need to understand.

c) Observing our criticisms of and projection on to others

If we ask ourselves what characteristics we find most distasteful in others, the list will contain many clues to our own shadow. What we see in others is often a reflection of our own mind that we project on to another. Our projection, if not addressed, transforms our environment and the people in it. Our environment then reflects the image we have created, and we risk becoming isolated.

We have created a reality that does not represent the world as it is (with its balance of good and bad) but one in which the world's faults and problems (reflections of our own shadow) become dominant in our thinking.

We separate ourselves from reality and move out of the present moment into a future state of expectation. These future events or situations are pure fanciful imagination and can never happen.

If we hear ourselves thinking: 'if only he would do this or that…' or 'If she could just be like this or that…' or 'If only they would understand where I was coming from…' this is our shadow speaking to us. Here we have yet another opportunity for deep examination and to come to terms with the shadow's inescapable existence.

It is critical that we do this. If we do not, we will create a vicious cycle: our projections and feelings of ill-will about others and the world become so ingrained *that we actually bring about that which we project.*

We are so imbued with the negative perception we have of others that they eventually do become negative to us. They have responded to our negative and defensive vitriol. We have triggered their 'defensive' ego and provoked their shadow projection on to us.

This vicious cycle of ill-will is then perpetuated until we have the courage to confront our ego and our shadow. Only then can we start the process of rechannelling, transformation and integration into a new wholeness.

As William Blake so rightly observes:

> If the fool would persist in his folly, he would become wise.

The sooner the better!

d) Observing our impulsive, 'accidental' slips

Sometimes we may respond very rapidly to an impulse and either say or do something that we subsequently realize was unnecessary, unkind or plain stupid. This is where we can also detect the presence of the shadow. Our subconscious dark side can manifest itself in an uncontrolled, unpremeditated manner. It says things that lie deep within us but which, in the normal course of our more controlled existence, we would never wish to say or do.

When we catch ourselves saying something and then thinking: 'Oh dear, I didn't mean to say that' or 'What was I thinking of when I did that?' or 'I don't know what got into me?', the shadow has overridden our conscious mind. This speech or action can be the result of a trigger, which we regret and feel ashamed of later, but sometimes it can be just spontaneous—for no apparent reason at all.

It is at moments such as these that we can perceive the workings of our shadow. The reason we said something spontaneous, unkind or unnecessary will reflect a repressed feeling. For example, if we were regularly criticised for being late as a child, we may have sublimated the concept of punctuality and repressed any feelings of sympathy towards untimeliness. So when someone arrives a few moments late for an appointment, we might say sarcastically and heatedly: 'You're late again! What was it this time? An accident I hope…'

Our repressed shadow slipped out with a hurtful and unnecessary additional comment. Of course, punctuality is a good thing and being late is disrespectful and irritating to others. But when the desire for timeliness becomes so strong that it leads to a toxic outburst, then clearly the virtue of being on time has become an unhelpful vice. We did not mean to be so harsh. It just came out.

Observing such unguarded remarks or actions and taking note of them will help us to uncover important aspects of our shadow.

e) Observing the same negative effect we have on different people as a result of our behaviour

When our behaviour prompts several people to react uncomfortably to us in the same way, this is a strong signal that our shadow is triggering a negative response that we would do well to understand and address.

This could be the result of our manner (too formal, too casual, too arrogant or too timid), our behaviour (too dismissive, too accepting, too disrespectful, too sycophantic) or our actions (too flaky, frequently changing plans at the last minute, not being grateful for favours, not being truthful, not recognising others, being selfish, being evasive, gossiping). The list of possibilities will be very long.

Understanding why such a reaction is taking place is the key to modifying (or even abandoning) the behaviour. To understand requires listening actively to any comments made, observing body language and noticing the corresponding behaviour. Asking for feedback is always good—given it is requested openly, humbly and without defensiveness or aggression.

For example, if we sense or are told by someone that they feel uncomfortable with us because they never know what we are feeling or whether we are enthusiastic about something or not, this is a signal that we are not open with our feelings or do not convey our views assertively enough. Our interlocutors are left confused and, therefore, troubled. This is both our ego and our shadow manifesting our repressed fear of being found wanting, wrong or overly keen to the point of being naïve or stupid.

f) Asking for feedback

Because behaviour can only be explained in relation to another, it always makes sense (as we suggested earlier in this chapter) to ask for feedback. This requires courage and openness of spirit. We also have to be willing to listen—without interruption, without trying to defend anything, without denial or anger. The best feedback will come from those who know us best, have a high level of emotional stability, empathy and maturity and have our interest at heart.

Asking them to serve as our mirror—to express how they honestly feel about our behaviour and the reactions they have to various characteristics we demonstrate—will prove invaluable to genuinely open mind. Although simple to explain, this is really difficult to accomplish well! It necessitates goodwill in equal measure in both parties. If we give any sense that we are being defensive, in denial or distrust the feedback, we will wreck the process immediately. It will then be very difficult to get back on course.

However, done well, soliciting feedback from those we trust gives a wonderful insight into the workings of our ego, our shadow and our capacity for toxicity. If we do not listen to or take heed of the feedback, nothing will change. We will remain unaware of the lessons that we can learn or the potential that we truly have.

If we do heed the call, change direction and break habits that have not served us well, we open the way for reconciling ourselves to our shadow and integrating it into our psyche. As a result, we will build trust and cultivate better relationships through more honest self-awareness and direct, unashamed, guilt-free communication. We will unearth and develop dormant, repressed talents, discover hidden gems of possibility and release strengths to accomplish our purpose in life and contribute to the growth of consciousness in humanity as a whole.

The shadow, paradoxically, comprises both darkness and valuable pointers to the direction of the light. There is much that is positive in what is hidden in the shadow. Enormous energy is trapped in the repressed, anxiety-ridden feelings, emotions, qualities, talents and abilities that were deemed unhelpful at some stage but could now be invaluable.

Take for example, a person's artistic abilities that have been repressed because considered too 'lightweight' or 'effete'—as in 'Our family doesn't do that'—but which, when re-examined in a new light, could result in a magnificent talent being released. Many people will have been told, as they grew up, that they were not 'good enough' for this or that and thus repressed their belief in themselves and given up any ambition. Examining the shadow may uncover the gifts that were pushed down.

Moreover, the shadow never lies, whereas ego lies all the time! The shadow tells us the honest truth about ourselves—should we be willing to face it. And if we can, the learning is without compare. Our objective must be for us to establish a creative relationship with our shadow. It will always be there. But instead of leading us into trouble through denial, fear or lack of observance, it can be the light that illuminates our path.

When addressed humbly and courageously and the darkness of the shadow is bathed in light, the tension and conflict within us is released and a sense of peace envelops us. We have learnt to accept ourselves better and freed ourselves from feelings of shame and guilt. We now know how to defuse negative emotions that erupt unexpectedly and to recognize more easily the sentiments we project on others. In recognising our shadow, we have acknowledged our self.

Shakespeare has Prospero say something similar in *The Tempest*. Prospero sees Caliban as deformed, rough, uncouth, distasteful. However, it is Prospero who has created Caliban in his own image and he represents, in many ways, the magician's own shadow. It is only at the end of the play that Prospero is able to speak this plainly, saying: 'This thing of darkness I acknowledge mine.'

We have faced our demons and learnt to own our disowned self. We are whole again and at peace. This is our awakening.

As Liz Greene so wonderfully writes:

> It is the suffering, crippled side of the personality which is both the dark shadow that won't change and also the redeemer that transforms one's life and alters one's values. The redeemer can get the hidden treasure or win the princess or slay the dragon because he's marked in some way—he's abnormal. The shadow is both the awful thing that needs redemption, and the suffering redeemer who can provide it.

The discovery and understanding of our own internal *personal shadow,* and the brutally honest, painful, patient, difficult but necessary shadow work to expose it, is the essential first step. Ultimately, it is the only way to finding solutions to the greater, more dangerous, more cataclysmic *collective shadow*—the source of the world's greatest toxicity and its greatest disasters.

vii) Are we able and willing to make decisions and take accountability for them?

There are a couple of separate but connected aspects here. The first is how willing are we to make decisions and how do we make them. The second issue is if we are prepared to be accountable for them.

Do we find it easy to make decisions or do we prevaricate anxiously? Do we make decisions about our lives sensibly—looking at pros and cons and the impact on others? Or do we tend to shoot from the hip, trusting our instincts and our emotions? Do we make decisions with others and seek their inputs? Or do we tend to go ahead without any consultation? Do we prefer not to make any decisions at all if we can help it, leaving it to others to make them?

There is no fixed way to make a decision. Each method has the potential for creating toxicity if it is not appropriate to the circumstances.

People who make decisions too quickly often make the wrong ones. However, sometimes it is necessary to make rapid decisions. There is no point in thinking too long when the house is on fire or a child is about to cross the road without looking. But quick decision-making can cause immense problems and be highly toxic. People who are prone to making rapid, ill-considered decisions need to learn patience. This is the essential virtue that helps us steer a more harmonious course and avoid disasters. As Lao Tzu observed:

> Simplicity, patience, compassion, these three are your greatest treasures.

Patience is not only vital to allow time for reflection, but it is also critical for enabling others to be engaged, inspired and committed. Patience is an essential quality in any leader. Equally, learning to 'sleep on it' has its value. The subconscious mind will often unravel the problem and make the decision more obvious the next morning.

On the other extreme, people who take too long—anxiously debating within themselves, unsure of what to do and frequently changing their minds—will almost always end up with a sub-optimal result. They will have undoubtedly missed endless opportunities along the way. In the words of Samuel Johnson:

> Nothing will ever be attempted if all possible objections must be first overcome.

Worse still, this potentially toxic behaviour will infuriate those who need a decision to be made—as well as those who have been consulted. Those who might be able to help will feel that their views are not valued and will soon lose interest.

These will often be people who when asked a question, for example, where they might like to eat, will turn it around and ask the interlocutor to make the decision. This will not be out of a sense of participation, but because they are frightened to make a decision. The problem is that this creates toxicity by signalling a lack of interest or enthusiasm.

If you are such a person, practise making decisions. This can be done by starting on small choices and deliberately taking a chance on the outcome.

Knowing and saying what you want is itself a decision. Doing this will make the person asking feel that there is some enthusiasm and commitment in the reply. There is nothing more disappointing than being told 'I don't know; you decide' every time you make a suggestion.

This habit or trait may well indicate that the person does not wish to take responsibility for their decision, should it prove to be wrong. Such a person should examine this carefully and its source (see triggers and shadows above, especially in vi).) It could well be that, as a child, they were criticised and slighted for making wrong judgements or told they were 'hopeless' at making decisions. They have thus been conditioned to avoid them!

The truth of the matter is that we all make mistakes. Mistakes are how we learn. Anyone who never makes a mistake never takes a risk and, as a result, never grows. It is better to take a risk, make a decision, get it wrong, and then learn from the mistake, than to never make a decision at all! In the words attributed to Theodore Roosevelt:

> In any moment of decision, the best thing you can do is the right thing, the next best thing is the wrong thing, and the worst thing you can do is nothing.

Making decisions correctly also requires us to take full responsibility and be accountable for their consequences. This is true of life. Our life is in our hands. We have the power to choose in which direction we wish to travel and accept responsibility for it. We have the power to be the hero or heroine of our own adventure—if we always own our decisions completely. This is our ultimate freedom. It is an extraordinary privilege and one that requires reflection, courage and determination. Freedom is not something to give away to anyone or to lose by default out of laziness or ignorance. Rather it is a gift to treasure and protect… always.

> Freedom makes a huge requirement of every human being. With freedom comes responsibility. For the person who is unwilling to grow up, the person who does not want to carry his own weight, this is a frightening prospect.
>
> —Eleanor Roosevelt

viii) Are we willing to ask for forgiveness and to forgive those who hurt us? Are we willing to show our vulnerable side?

Having observed our ego and shadow, we realize that we are not perfect. We have faults and failings and are fully capable of being insensitive, unkind and cruel. Do we now have the courage to ask for forgiveness and to forgive those who are unkind to us?

Asking for forgiveness, genuinely and sincerely, is an act of contrition and humility that immediately reduces toxicity—especially in ourselves. It is an act that reconciles the various aspects of our psyche and recreates a sense of wholeness. It releases stress and anxiety and is, indeed, divine. Alexander Pope captured this sentiment in his famous maxim:

> To err is human, to forgive divine.

And in many religions, the importance of forgiving and asking for forgiveness is well recognized.

> 'Do not judge, and you will not be judged. Do not condemn and you will not be condemned. Forgive, and you will be forgiven.'
>
> —Luke 6:37

In Buddha's teachings, forgiveness is what puts an end to hostility and animosity, for which the Pali word is *vera*, but which we might also call toxicity. Forgiveness eliminates the idea of winning or losing and opens the way to freedom from ego and peace.

Islam teaches that if someone sincerely asks for forgiveness, the wronged person should forgive him:

> A kind and courteous word and forgiveness are better than the charity that is followed by abuse.
>
> —Qur'an, 2:263

Are we fully prepared to ask for forgiveness for the wrong we may have done to another? Or do we prefer to ignore, deny and dismiss our toxicity whenever it rears its ugly head?

Similarly, are we willing to forgive others? This does not mean condoning, excusing or even forgetting the wrongdoing, but rather letting go of any grudges or bitterness. Not forgiving is the poison that invades our body and mind. It courses through our system night and day, with known serious unhealthy physical and mental consequences.

If we allow negative feelings to crowd out positive ones, we risk drowning in unhealed anger, resentment and bitterness. We exacerbate toxicity rather than calming it.

To usefully manage toxicity through forgiveness, we can follow the exercises below. Sincerity is always key.

a) Practise apologizing properly and honestly. We should learn not to say 'sorry' in an insincere, mechanical way, but imagine and ask ourselves: How is the other person feeling? This is to practise putting ourselves in another's shoes and to acknowledge that we have hurt them.

b) Do not be frightened of asking for forgiveness, rather than just saying sorry. Asking for forgiveness is an admission of wrongdoing, but also an offer of reconciliation. It is an acceptance of responsibility and a demonstration of vulnerability. It should be done without making excuses.

However, we need to remember that we cannot force anyone to forgive us. They need to decide for themselves whether they wish to do so or not. But we can always treat others with empathy and compassion and simply do our sincere best.

c) In forgiving others, we need to be sure to make it *our* choice to do this and not the result of being a 'victim'. We should never feel coerced into forgiving others for the sake of buying time or a moment of peace. In taking responsibility for forgiving—and doing so honestly and truthfully because we wish to—we regain our power and automatically move from suffering to forgiveness. We may not have reduced the toxicity of others, but we have certainly managed our own.

d) Forgiveness is about *our* spiritual healing—regaining our wholeness, self-confidence and self-worth. It is about *our* health, sanity and happiness. It should never be about trying to control or change another through some form of confused manipulation, such as telling another we forgive them when in fact we do not. Such dishonesty is the work of ego and shadow and, far from reducing toxicity, only serves to exacerbate it.

e) Forgiving, asking for forgiveness and being vulnerable are beautiful acts of self-awareness and humaneness. They are born of kindness, compassion and love. As the word implies, *for-giving* is an act of giving. The gift is of love. Being honest and truthful about our actions and carefully considering their impact on others will enable us to create opportunities for reconciliation. It will stimulate open communication and allow us to form deep, mutually enhancing relationships—to the benefit of all.

ix) Are we willing to ask for help?

Part of showing our vulnerable side is our capacity for being willing to ask for help. This is not meant to suggest handing over responsibility to others for things we should be doing ourselves. That would be laziness. Rather it means acknowledging that, in the complex and often confused world in which we live, we cannot resolve everything on our own. To imagine so is unrealistic and unwise, not to say potentially reckless. We all need help of one sort or another.

The problem arises when we believe—and our ego pride encourages us to believe—that we are an independent and self-sufficient fortress. We are perfectly capable of managing everything on our own, thank you! If we allow pride (the false belief that asking for help is demeaning or an indication of weakness) to get in the way of common sense, that is toxic behaviour. It is also unhelpful—especially when it is obvious help is required and that delaying will only make things worse.

Asking for help is another way to engage collaboratively and compassionately with another. It opens doors and creates opportunities for good relationships and mutual support. It is respectful of the talents of others and recognizes them. Toxicity cannot coexist with an honest and humble request for help.

x) Do we find it easy to recognize and thank others? And are we gracious and comfortable accepting thanks?

It is the little gestures, expressed with sincerity and warmth, that mean the most. And yet these simple acts of kindness, which do so much to defuse toxicity and create the right environment, seem often to be forgotten or dismissed in today's time-constrained and automated life. Just a smile, a quick but sincere 'thank you', and a signal of genuine appreciation all send out positive vibrations that help create the right environment.

Research by employee recognition expert Christopher Littlefield found that while the vast majority of people (88%) associate being praised with feeling valued, nearly the same number (77%) also associate being recognized with discomfort or embarrassment!

Recognising others and thanking them for what they do to help us is a manifestation of goodness. It builds trust and confidence—both in the giver and the receiver. Both giver and receiver can benefit hugely from this demonstration of connection that uplifts, motivates and endears. Human beings are creatures of emotion and the emotion of feeling wanted, appreciated and loved is primordial. Recognising and thanking taps into that essential emotion and literally lifts the spirits.

However, giving and receiving thanks has to be done sensitively and carefully. It is important to learn to do this well.

When *giving* thanks, we should:

a) be totally authentic, avoiding jokes or asides of any kind;

b) be clear about what we are being thankful for, which demonstrates that we have thought about the service rendered and reinforces our authenticity;

c) be specific about the 'how' of what has been achieved as much as the 'what'—explaining the way in which the achievement was conducted, the care and time given, as well as the end result, the 'what';

d) be open about how we feel about the achievement and the effect this has had on us personally.

Recognising and thanking others may sometimes seem trivial and not worth the effort, but nothing could be further from the truth. *Not* recognising is, in itself, toxic because it creates disquiet, disappointment and disharmony. Disheartened people soon lose interest and enthusiasm, and everyone suffers as a consequence.

> There is nothing which I can esteem more highly than being and appearing grateful. For this one virtue is not only the greatest, but is also the parent of all the other virtues.
>
> —Cicero

> Oh Lord that lends me life,
> Lend me a heart replete with thankfulness!
>
> —William Shakespeare,
> *Henry VI, Part 2*

Knowing how to *accept* thanks and recognition is similarly vital. This should also be done gracefully and sincerely. People who find it hard to accept thanks often do so out of self-deprecation or a desire to be or seem modest. We are conditioned not to vaunt our successes or to appear immodest. But we also have to be mindful of the impact that such a muted response may have on the person doing the thanking. The thanks giver has made themselves a little bit vulnerable by offering a 'gift' and may have had to overcome their own shyness or pride in offering their thanks.

Not responding positively and clearly can thus be very hurtful to the thanks giver. It is as if a gift has been refused (not a physical gift, but a gift nevertheless). The giver wants to see the recipient appreciate, enjoy, even savour the moment.

An appropriate response is to show suitable pride—but not arrogance. It is also good to express how uplifting and motivational the recognition is. Lastly, any others who have participated in the process can also be mentioned.

It should be clear now that giving and receiving thanks is an opportunity for building growth and goodwill. Equally, not doing this well—due to sheer indifference, insensitivity or inadequate understanding—can create or exacerbate toxicity. To reflect on how we perform in this area, we can carefully and honestly reflect (or seek trusted feedback) on these questions:

a) Do we understand the importance of thanking and recognising others and doing so properly?

b) Do we find it easy to do and, if not, how do we plan to develop this skill?

c) Are we comfortable acknowledging the help that others give us? Is it easy for us to do so?

d) Are we aware of the impact that not thanking may have on the person performing the service?

e) Do we take for granted or dismiss what others do for us as something that is expected or normal, not requiring recognition?

f) How comfortable are we are receiving thanks or recognition?

g) How well and completely do we share any thanks received with colleagues, recognising their part in any achievement?

xi) How generous are we really?

> The Master has no possessions.
> The more he does for others, the happier he is.
> The more he gives to others, the wealthier he is.
>
> —Lao Tzu, Tao Te Ching,
> as interpreted by Stephen Mitchell

> Lord teach me to be generous … To give and not to count the cost.
>
> —St Ignatius of Loyola

Human generosity is a quality that goes back to our earliest origins when survival depended on collaboration and sharing. Those who were willing to give (in whatever form) found they were rewarded with a feeling of delight and happiness. We now know this is due to the feel-good hormone dopamine released in the brain. They also discovered that their act of generosity often resulted in a reciprocal act and the establishment of a mutually satisfying relationship.

However, there were those who could not go along with this empathetic self-sacrifice for the good of the group. They did not understand how generosity had so many secondary benefits once the initial selfish benefit of keeping for oneself was overcome. We can hypothesise that the extremely mean tended to seal their own fate. Their meanness created toxicity in the group, which resulted in their being rejected and excluded. However, it is also clear that modern humans have both generous and mean sides.

Why we might be more or less inclined to be generous depends on both our 'natural' instinct (genetics) and 'nurture' (how we have been brought up). Almost everyone has a generous side, but individual motivations, values and triggers vary considerably.

It is reasonable to assume that human beings are born with a predisposition for generosity—if only because this is linked to self-interest and survival. This can be seen when very small children naturally share their toys with others, before the concept of 'me' and 'mine' has developed. If they live in an environment that encourages them to be generous of spirit—to give without expecting anything in return and experience the happiness of giving—then they will most likely carry these values into their formative years and mature into empathetic, generous adults. (This is covered in more detail in *The Stairway to Happiness.*)

The person who buys a sandwich or a coffee for the homeless person, who supports good causes or who voluntarily helps those in need has developed their empathetic side and been taught that giving and caring is part of being a good human being. They have learnt to differentiate between 'logic'—which introduces an assessment of benefit and loss to themselves—and 'empathy'—which brings into the equation the altruistic dimension of the desire to do good.

However, if they have been conditioned to view acts of generosity as resulting primarily in personal loss, then they will not be generous as a matter of preference. They will believe that 'security' and the protection of their own wealth has a higher value than giving to others. They may also view 'charity' as the responsibility of government or philanthropists. The result will be they are likely to be mean and stingy in their everyday dealings.

Meanness and stinginess are significant contributors to toxicity because they upset the harmony of the group. They create asymmetric relationships—whereby one party gives much more than the other. Asymmetrical relationships never work out because they are *in their nature* toxic and cause irritation, resentment and anger.

> With gentleness, overcome anger.
> With generosity, overcome meanness.
> With truth, overcome delusion.
>
> —The Dhammapada,
> rendered by Thomas Byrom

Generosity should be treasured as a profound act of kindness when it is not self-serving, is without ego and expressed sincerely. Generosity builds trust and positive connections. Its absence has the opposite effect.

To understand generosity in ourselves, we need to reflect sincerely on the following questions:

a) What do we mean by generosity? Do we predominantly mean money?

b) To what extent would we consider ourselves to be generous?

c) How would others (our friends) describe us? Generous, normal, tight or very tight?

d) When giving, do we feel more that we have lost something, or that we have gained something?

e) How mindful are we of our tendency to have an initial impulse to give, only to have second thoughts and pull back?

f) Are we generally the first, the last, or somewhere in the middle when it comes to 'picking up the bill'?

g) How conscious are we that the consistent absence of generosity creates toxicity?

xii) What constitutes a good relationship for us? What are we looking for? Why are relationships often so toxic?

We all seek and aspire to good relationships. We look especially for one that will 'complete' us, make us whole. We hope and believe that the ideal partner exists. Somewhere out there is the person with whom we will be able to share our life and live happily with for the rest of our lives.

We believe our fulfilment is dependent on an external somebody. We think our hopes and dreams will be delivered by that somebody with whom we will have a perfect life and overcome all obstacles that might arise.

Unfortunately, our dependence on someone else to enable us to become whole and our seeking the right person (combined with the implication that this will happen in the future) are the very reasons why such relationships can never be truly established. We are harbouring a dangerous delusion that will likely lead to disappointment and suffering—and much toxicity in the process.

Our desires, cravings and seeking come from a primary ego urge—originally designed to ensure survival of the human race! It expresses itself initially through a powerful sexual charge, the erotic attraction to and from the partner. This is the libido that constitutes for Freud the motivating force behind all human activity, as well as the seeking of pleasure and sexual fulfilment.

The problem is that this biologically necessary cycle (craving followed by temporary satisfaction, followed by more craving and more temporary satisfaction) creates the illusion that the satisfaction of real wholeness can be achieved by someone or something outside of ourselves. When applied to life in general these objects of desire become 'must haves', which we then chase for the rest of our lives.

This chase after the perfect relationship, though, is an illusion—a figment of our imagination that is always out there, in the future. And the future never comes! We are looking for happiness and wholeness in someone who exists as an *object* we desire. We believe they will fulfil our needs. If not, we can change and mould them as necessary. We also labour under the false assumption that the other party is looking for the exact same things in the same way and will conform to our image of them. The fact is that object of our dream is a person in their own right. They have their own dreams, material, emotional and spiritual needs, opinions, ambitions and expectations.

Herein lies the core of the problem. It is small wonder that so many relationships and marriages founder in a storm of toxicity. The initial falling-in-love phase—with its ego-free total acceptance, forgiveness, nurturing and protection of the other—is a glimpse into wholeness. But the relationship turns into drama and suffering as both partners come to the realisation that the other does not fit the (illusory) image they had of them—and has no wish to do so.

As long as both parties provide each other with what they want (typically in the early part of the relationship) they feel loved, loving and are kind, considerate and generous towards each other. However, once either party stops receiving what they want, they begin to feel rejected, unloved and disappointed. Ego then steps into the fray. It employs its well-rehearsed attack and defence mechanisms: blaming, complaining, lying, arguing, bullying, gaslighting, provoking and all manner of emotional and sometimes physical violence.

Because each partner sees themself as a separate entity and is trying to find fulfilment from what is external, they now need to try to control the other person. This always fails. Seeking to coerce another and bend them to our will—to obtain love the way we want it in accordance with the image we have created—is a recipe for suffering and pain. This dependence for fulfilment on another based on a division between ourselves and the other leads to an oscillation between happiness and misery, between love and hate. It is a war that cannot be won by either party. Unfortunately, it is also the perfect toxic mixture.

True love has no opposite. The concept of hate cannot exist with real love. Love is complete in itself and is not dependent on anything or anybody. Love is our essential nature. It is only through deep reflection and an understanding of *who we really are* that we can overcome such toxic relationships.

And here we are back again with the need to spend quiet, patient, honest and occasionally painful time reflecting deeply on who we really are. We have to look at how our ego operates and what our shadow contains. This is the only way to eliminate any notion of toxicity. We must elevate our consciousness and rediscover our truth and our natural, pre-conditioned goodness.

8

Regaining Our Power—the Key to Managing Toxicity

We often refer to 'toxic events' or 'toxic people'. However, we should be careful to understand that events are themselves neutral and 'toxic people' do not necessarily mean us any harm. By labelling a person (or situation) toxic, we are pigeonholing and prejudging. These are both acts of toxicity because we are automatically perceiving the person in a more negative way than may be warranted. A position that closes off options for resolution.

It is interesting to observe how people react to an unexpected and undesired event, such as a missed flight connection or an 'objectionable' co-traveller. Those whose instant reaction is to view these as toxic are likely to make the situation worse for themselves and for everyone else. Their attitude alone—often due to some previous travel experiences and beliefs about airlines and fellow travellers—means they are negatively prejudging, which allows their ego ('How could anyone do this to *me*?') to be triggered. They have lost the battle with themselves before anything has even started! It is *their* preconceptions and prejudices that are creating the toxicity and these are at fault.

Those who are aware of their triggers and have learnt to view life as an adventure are much more likely to find a calmer and happier way to manage the various forms of toxicity. They understand that life is by nature ever-changing, uncertain and insecure—that is what gives it its excitement and joy. In contrast, those who have rigid expectations will react negatively when things do not happen as expected.

Regaining power over ourselves and hence over toxic events or people requires a flexibility of mind and a generally more positive, accepting and amenable outlook on life. Power comes to those who have learnt not to take themselves too seriously and have a more wholesome understanding of human nature and how the world works. Such people are more apt to let things that do not matter pass and to let go of any need to control what cannot be controlled. They will not allow themselves to become involved or implicated in battles that cannot be won. They save their energy for when something genuinely important occurs, something that they *are* able to influence—especially if that pertains to their own behaviour.

Because they are more aware of themselves—meaning who they really are—they have developed greater self-confidence and are better able to rise above potential issues and remain level-headed. They have brought forth and faced what is 'within', rather than allow what is 'within' to destroy them.

> Jesus said, 'That which you have will save you if you bring it forth from yourselves. That which you do not have within you will kill you if you do not have it within you.'
>
> —The Gospel of Thomas, Saying 70

The ability to recognize, understand and manage our own thoughts and emotions is fundamental to gaining power over toxic situations and toxic people. Recognizing what is going on inside ourselves—being able to detect and interpret our mental and physical signals and triggers—is the source of immense power. We are in charge of our destiny. We understand our own reactions and actions. We determine our future because our thinking is 'right thinking'. We do not react to toxicity because we do not need to. And we do not need to because we can see it coming. Like the martial arts practitioner, we know how to deflect the blow and avoid it hurting us.

Understanding why we feel the way we do and why we behave in a particular way are the starting points for changing our own behaviour and for regaining our power. This understanding and self-control give us the freedom to create and choose between different options. Previously, we had no choice but to respond automatically via the knee-jerk reaction of our subconscious mind and unconscious ego. Regaining our power means taking full responsibility for our thoughts and our actions. We no longer blame anyone for what happens—not even ourselves!

> He who blames others has a long way to go on his journey.
> He who blames himself is halfway there.
> He who blames no one has arrived.
>
> —Chinese proverb

Awareness of our feelings and emotions and being honest and truthful about them makes us better able to express them in an open, non-aggressive and non-submissive manner. This is the core of true assertiveness (and mirrors the Buddhist Middle Way of right thinking). This skill of assertiveness (covered in detail in chapter 15) is critical in managing toxicity. It requires openness and the ability to communicate diplomatically and compassionately but nevertheless clearly and unambiguously—especially under pressure.

9

Wholeness Regained

When any ego-derived structure dissolves it will, initially, cause suffering and pain. The same is true of the unlocking of ego's little brother or sister—the dark shadow of our repressed feelings.

Paradoxically, however, the dismantling of our ego and the illumination of our shadow transforms our self-awareness and awakens us to truth and honesty. This process allows the light to shine in and expose the toxicity within us for what it is.

Once exposed, our toxicity automatically loses its power and ceases to be. The wound can now begin to heal. We have regained our wholeness, our integrity and our power. We are now in a better state to help others manage their toxicity and regain their power too.

Now we can do this from a position of compassion, acceptance, understanding and love. This becomes our intention, our purpose and our calling.

PART 2

Strategies for Dealing with Toxic Situations and Toxic People

10

Introduction to Key Strategies

Part 1 undertook the necessary work of examining the component parts of toxicity. We not only looked at some of its many manifestations (such as in the workplace) but also the question of our own personal role and responsibility. How we are involved in creating and managing toxicity is often neglected but is vital to grasp if we are to tackle it. We can now usefully consider strategies for managing toxic people and situations—wherever and whenever they occur.

While every 'toxic' circumstance will be different, there are enough common features to be able to follow helpful strategies. Naturally, these need to be applied with sensitivity and discretion. The following chapters focus on each of the *seven Key Strategies for dealing with toxicity.*

The seven Key Strategies are:

1) *Recognize toxicity early and avoid* if you can. Do not be drawn in. Protect yourself.
2) *Master yourself.* Know your power. Know who you really are.
3) *Stay calm. Do not react.* Stay open, present and aware.
4) *Set boundaries.* Know what you can and cannot control.
5) *Be assertive.* Learn assertiveness skills, be sincere, use humour (carefully).
6) *Focus on solutions.*
7) *Build great relationships.*

11

Key Strategy 1: Recognize Toxicity Early and Avoid It

Beware of being drawn in. Protect yourself!

The first important strategic learning is to be aware of toxicity and recognize it whenever it rears its ugly head. This is essential to avoid being unwittingly caught off guard and drawn in.

Toxicity arises in many forms and with varying levels of velocity, as we have shown in Part 1. Its forms include: violent and immediate; hypnotic and initially seductive; or a slow but deadly poison. Furthermore, toxic people come in all shapes, sizes and ages. They may be only occasionally toxic—when themselves triggered or stressed—or more generally toxic, with deeper, more fundamental problems.

Thoroughly digesting, and then applying the learnings of Part 1 will have made this process easier but eternal vigilance remains the watchword. Whatever way toxicity appears, be alert, recognize its presence and be prepared.

As we explored in Chapter 5, it is very helpful to always keep in mind that a state of toxicity will only affect us *if we allow it to.* It is often very difficult to avoid being affected, which is why we have developed the seven strategies. But the fact remains that toxicity cannot affect us unless we allow it to draw us in and trigger us. We *always* have the power to deal with toxicity before it energises us. And we should not hesitate to use our power! It will spare us much suffering and even save our life

The Zen expert DT Suzuki was masterful in not allowing toxicity to unbalance him. He would consciously recognize a potentially toxic trap and then tactfully and diplomatically deflect it. Intellectual, congenial, simple and gifted with a subtle sense of humour and great compassion, Suzuki would defuse likely toxic situations with wisdom and compassion. He would be sure to leave the other party with their self-respect undamaged.

On one occasion, Suzuki was confronted by a student who was mischievously seeking to create a toxic exchange between him and another renowned Buddhist scholar, Professor Junjiro Takakusu. Being acutely aware of the propensity for 'sages' to suffer from ego-derived one-upmanship (unfortunately fairly common in spiritual and religious circles) and that there are no absolute truths, Suzuki never sought to defend his position or argue. (As soon as one feels defensive, we can be sure ego is present!) When the student challenged him in open session by stating that Professor Takakusu held a different position from Suzuki on several scholastic points, he gave it a brief moment of consideration. Then he simply said, calmly and with a gentle smile on his face:

'This is a very big world; there is plenty of room in it for both Professor Takakusu and me.'

By the simple mechanism of shifting the narrative and deftly and tactfully avoiding any potential toxicity, the risk of conflict was immediately dissolved. And this was accomplished with no loss of face to anyone.

When we are assailed with opinions that differ from our own—especially from people who may not be intent on listening to an answer or who are convinced that they are right—we are under no obligation to be drawn in. Sometimes keeping silent and avoiding any response is the best strategy. The aphorism often attributed to Mark Twain expresses this wittily:

> Never argue with stupid people, they will drag you down to their level and then beat you with experience.

In all interpersonal contexts, there are always (at least) two people involved, and *both* have a role to play in any interaction. It is very easy to be drawn in to the unhealthy game being played by the toxic person. Our ego gets triggered and then we re-act in like manner—dragging us down to the same level of unconsciousness as the aggressor.

Ego needs and relishes conflict, tension, defence and attack. Ego creates conflict to justify and reinforce the illusion of the false sense of identity. It needs to constantly prove its validity and existence. Re-acting simply fuels the fire of antagonism. It makes it harder to find resolution, as both parties go headlong into battle. Any remnants of calmness or conscious awareness are violently brushed aside by the toxicity. Once a toxic situation takes hold, suffering and pain are inescapable.

However, you should not conclude that *all* arguments and disagreements are bad. Or that defending a position or point of view is not sometimes appropriate. On the contrary, having the courage to express our opinion is the mark of a free society, which we should do all we can to respect, protect and nurture. We should encourage people to put forward their thoughts and defend their right to do so.

This expression must be in the spirit of openness and with the genuine desire to discover wisdom and truth. In this case, it is highly desirable and the only way to advance knowledge.

We are contrasting this spirit of openness with the situation where arguments and disagreements are raised without respect and without the willingness to listen to another's opinion. In a toxic situation, there is no acceptance of proper debate, no possibility of anyone changing their mind.

When there is no spirit of openness and discovery, even mature people with balanced personalities can easily allow themselves to become 'unconscious'. Through being unwary, they plunge headfirst into the trap set by the toxic person's ego. The triggered toxicity of uncontrolled egos, which do not wish to give in or appear to lose, becomes the cause of most of the serious incidents in the world—from heated arguments and domestic violence to murder and even wars. The all too rapid reaction to the psychotic and delusionary demands of an untamed and uncontrolled ego can lead to death or a lifetime of guilt and remorse.

Toxicity is also often experienced in a less immediate and violent way, but, as we observed above, is more manipulative and subtle. Ego has endless crafty ways of infiltrating the mind—even of saints and sages. In fact, kind, well-meaning souls are particularly vulnerable, and can easily allow themselves to be drawn into the skilful predator's toxic game. Habitual predators are skilful because they are likely to have been at the game for a long time—maybe even from childhood. Like a proficient chess player, they know all the moves.

In a laudable effort to be sympathetic and helpful, the well-meaning person may seek to help the toxic person who is busy doing their 'poor me' routine. The kind, yet unwary person may show sympathy and start to agree with the toxic person about their problems and how unfortunate they are. They may then go on to collaborate in general negativity and gossip—in order not to offend, to avert conflict or simply to please.

Unless they have considerable self-awareness alongside their empathy, before long the well-meaning person gets dragged down and begins to drown in a whirlpool of toxicity. They are left feeling depressed, unloved, forlorn and unhappy, wondering how on earth they got there.

This is even more acutely painful if the person is close to us, such as a family member, or if we have formed a romantic attachment to them and harbour understandable hopes of a loving, lifelong relationship.

Faced with the toxic 'poor me', some may be tempted to step in and help the 'victim'. While again well-meaning, this is fraught with danger. Such help requires real (professional) skill. It can easily become a time-consuming and mentally demanding obligation from which it may be difficult to extricate oneself. Why? Because any attempt to extricate oneself will be met by a response from the toxic person that they are being 'abandoned' and let down in their moment of greatest need. This is something toxic people will be very quick to bring up in order to provoke deep feelings of guilt.

The negativity of toxic people can easily overwhelm, leading to feelings of despondency as well as exhaustion. Power is effectively transferred to the toxic person and the victim enters a depressing kind of prison.

The fact is that toxic people do not respect the feelings or needs of others. Toxicity is essentially selfish. It drains others of their time and energy. We should be very aware that toxic people will drain us of our energy too—should we be unwise enough to allow them to. Our happiness is in our hands and no one else's.

It is our responsibility to hold and exercise our power in such a way as to remain in charge of our life. Exercise that power carefully, compassionately and fully. Use it with conscious, open and present awareness at all times.

Hence our first piece of practical advice, when we have learned to recognize some of the manifestations of toxicity:

Do not be drawn into toxic situations and keep well clear of toxic people if you possibly can!

This may seem like a cop-out but it is very sound advice. It will save many hours of wasted, frustrating, energy-sapping heartache—as those who have been sucked into the quicksand of toxicity will readily attest.

Having the intuition to recognize toxicity and toxic people is the first important step. And the second is as soon as you do sense that you are in the presence of toxicity, just keep away.

Do not engage. Do not get stuck emotionally. *If you allow yourself an emotional connection of more than ten seconds, you will be stuck.* And ego will arise. Just be polite, make your excuse if you must, and move on swiftly.

This, of course, does not mean we should abandon those who are genuinely in need of help, including friends and family. Here again, we should trust our instincts. However, when we do have an option, we should be very conscious that surrounding ourselves with negative, toxic people will imbue us with that same negativity and destroy our happiness—just as they have destroyed theirs. The lightness of our soul will rapidly become heavy and downbeat.

We will then attract more negativity towards us. Misery attracts misery. That is the Law of Attraction, which is immutable. If we send negative vibrations into the universe, they will connect with other negative vibrations and return to us in like form.

The toxicity we take on will also damage our other relationships. Friends will begin to turn away from us. Being 'dragged down' is also highly injurious to one's own health (mental and physical) and causes sickness. In short, you have better, happier things to do.

However, sometimes you will have a very good reason to enter the toxic fray—perhaps to help someone or because you are already in its midst. If so, we strongly recommend adopting the remaining six Key Strategies (each presented in its own chapter) to direct your journey in the most effective way possible.

Before we move on to the other strategies, we want to explore what is needed to heal the toxic person. And then, in the concluding part of this chapter, put this first strategy into the context of self-love, self-protection and purpose.

Before you decide to enter (or remain in) a toxic situation, you will need to become very aware of who you really are, and what your own toxicity is! (This is one of the main themes of Part 1.) Then you can tap into this powerful fount of knowledge at any time.

As you become stronger (strength in this context means wise), consciously aware and technically knowledgeable, you will be able to see beyond the deeply unhappy 'form' of the toxic person. Instead, you will feel a profound sense of sympathy for and compassion towards their suffering. It is *not* their soul that is behaving so dreadfully. Deep down, in their unconditioned and natural state, they are not toxic! Toxicity comes from their ego and their complete attachment to the false sense of self created by their ego, in which they have invested so much energy.

Toxic people are playing a role and acting it out so well that they have fallen in love with their image—just as Narcissus did in Greek mythology—and cannot break the spell this image has cast. Narcissus fell in love with his own reflection in a pool of water and stared at it for the remainder of his life.

Another mythological perspective is offered in Hinduism: life is essentially a game. The supreme spirit, Brahman, is present in everything and everywhere. This means it is also the Self, the 'I'-ness, of humans (known as Atman in Sanskrit). The Self manifests itself in every possible guise, including extreme toxicity! Every creature, including the toxic person, is an expression of Brahman—only they are not conscious of it. The role the toxic person is playing is one they may truly believe in. But it is just an act, a drama, a performance!

William Shakespeare captured this thought when he wrote in *As You Like It*:

> All the world's a stage,
> And all the men and women merely players.

Strange as it may often seem—but made explicit in Hindu and other philosophies—there is always a soul behind the actor lost in their performance. This soul in its natural, pre-conditioned state desires to be loved and wanted. Beyond ego, the toxic person is crying for help.

The problem is that they cannot access this better being themselves because they are trapped in their own prison. Believing an image of themselves that is unreal, they have shut out the light of truth. They are blocking their own path to redemption and damaging yours in the process.

> When another person makes you suffer, it is because he suffers deeply within himself, and his suffering is spilling over. He does not need punishment; he needs help. That's the message he is sending.
>
> —Thich Nhat Hanh

Until there is a crack in that unreal, egotistical persona, the light cannot shine through. They are condemned to live in this prison of their own making—unaware that the key is in their pocket. They can never be free in the sense of being free of conditioned illusions and unreal expectations.

If the toxic person is fortunate, they may have a nervous breakdown or other medical problem that requires them to radically rethink who they are and what their purpose is. This 'way of the cross' may result in revelations about themselves that force them to observe their ego and confront their shadow. Ironically, this 'disaster' may be their salvation. Until then, there will always be something missing, some disquiet, a disconnection from Life and deep unhappy suffering. Inner peace will always prove elusive until they acquire the humility to learn and understand what is happening and why it is happening. Until they open their hearts and are willing to listen and actively surrender, they will not become properly conscious and will remain trapped.

If you are called to help and try to heal a toxic person, you should think hard before accepting such a challenge. Do you have the requisite skills and experience to undertake such a task? Much will also depend on your own inner strength and 'presence'. Do you believe the toxic person genuinely wishes to be helped? Or are they just using this as a pretext to gain (or regain) favour and establish (resume) their controlling and manipulative practices?

You will have to decide whether they are being honest and whether you are ready for this. If you conclude that they really are not genuine about being helped, there is very little you or anyone else can or should do. Simply withdraw gracefully. To do otherwise will be to waste time and energy.

If, however, they are truly sincere about wanting to be helped, then the very act of seeking help is itself an act of contrition, of humility and responsibility. It is a cause for celebration!

One last word of warning: Do not confuse the genuine cry for help with the toxicity of the skilful, manipulative 'poor me' masquerading as a reforming character. The two are often difficult to tell apart.

You will ultimately have to decide whether you wish to take this up yourself or whether you should suggest they consult an experienced professional. (If they are genuine, they should be open to the idea of obtaining professional help. Making such a suggestion will certainly test their sincerity!)

What is certain is that they will not resolve their toxicity or be able to become 'whole' and at peace only through their own efforts.

Toxicity, self-love, self-protection and purpose

Avoiding toxicity is not cowardice but common sense. It is an act of self-love in the sense that we are appreciating and respecting who we are—even if others are not. We have every right, as human beings, to have our own interests at heart. We should be able to focus on those things that will help us to grow and improve ourselves and live in harmony and peace.

Self-love also means letting go of those people who show no concern for us and infect or harm us with their negative thoughts and actions. We do not need to feel guilty *in any way* about stepping away from people whose negativity only depresses us. Misery loves company and miserable people have negative opinions about practically anything. Negative people celebrate failures and will find a negative slant even on successes. Hurt people hurt other people and seek to make others feel inadequate because they feel inadequate themselves.

Self-love means we can—and must—retain our power and self-respect by keeping away and not giving permission for others to belittle, bully or hurt us.

A couple of maxims (usually attributed to Eleanor Roosevelt and Gandhi) express this sentiment clearly:

> No one can hurt you without your consent.

> They cannot take away our self-respect if we do not give it to them.

If we are willing victims and give permission to others to abuse us, we are not respecting ourselves or showing ourselves the love we deserve. Self-love is empowerment and liberation. We should be careful to nurture, preserve and protect it. Our future depends on it. Or in the words attributed to Gandhi:

> The future depends on what you do today.

Self-love also requires us to ensure that whatever we do—whatever activities, roles or jobs we undertake—are ones that give us joy and satisfaction. This means having a *purpose* and a *passion* for something we really enjoy. This is not only a vital aspect of Life but also a clear expression of self-love.

Too many people just 'exist' because they are stuck in meaningless jobs. As a result, they leave their brains at the door of their office or workplace and cruise boringly through the day, living only for the weekend or a holiday. Living in the future is not living at all—since the future does not exist except as a thought. So when the weekend comes it will be another disappointment because the basic problem has not been addressed: the need to find a meaning to life.

Everyone needs to pay the bills but achieving this by doing things that mean nothing and are pure drudgery is a recipe for disaster and unhappiness. When we find our purpose, we become like a rock that will never break whatever waves crash against it. We empower ourselves to overcome any challenge that comes our way—however toxic the challenge might be. In the words of Friedrich Nietzsche:

> Those who have a 'why' to live for, can bear almost any 'how'.

It is not always easy to know what our purpose is. The way to discover it is to become aware of our thoughts and examine carefully and honestly what truly excites us. Look for what uplifts us, what we feel passionate about and what provides us with satisfaction and fulfilment. It is discovering the love that is inside us.

If we are in an occupation or profession that we dislike or working with people or a boss who are toxic, we should take time to find what we *do* enjoy. Then we can plan to transition to a different role, maybe in a different department, or even a different profession.

This may mean retraining or accepting an initially lower income or status. It absolutely does not have to be a sudden decision. We should not throw away what we currently have, or take a snap decision out of anger or frustration. That makes no sense and would be the reaction of unenlightened ego rather than maturity.

If, on mature reflection, we feel exhilarated by the prospect of change and doing what we know we love and enjoy most, we can plan a considered course of action to get us there. It is always the case that we do best what we enjoy doing most. By choosing to do what we enjoy, we dramatically increase the chances of finding 'success'. Success, in this context, means feeling a deep sense of fulfilment in the enjoyment of life.

> The meaning of life is just to be alive. It is so plain and so obvious and so simple. And yet, everybody rushes around in a great panic as if it were necessary to achieve something beyond themselves.
>
> —Alan Watts

Once our chosen path matches our true purpose we will experience even greater satisfaction. We will not need to go 'beyond ourselves' because we are already there. And we will find it that much easier to handle any toxicity that arises.

We have all been created for a reason and we all have a purpose to our existence—even if we do not yet know what it is. We simply have to find it and then have the courage to convert our idea into action. As soon as we discover our purpose in life, we will not only transform our own lives, but we will also transform the lives of others through our passion, our enthusiasm and our energy.

This is the blessed release from the desperate attachment and self-imposed need to satisfy the expectations of others. External pressures have dictated what we are 'expected' to do—rather than giving us the freedom to do what is right for us. This is true freedom. And when we act in this way, nobody can take away that freedom from us.

> It is this spiritual freedom—which cannot be taken away—that makes life meaningful and purposeful.
>
> —Viktor Frankl,
> *Man's Search for Meaning*

12

Key Strategy 2: Master Yourself

Know your power. Know who you really are.

The second Key Strategy (and the following ones) are designed to help you manage toxic people when you cannot avoid toxicity and must address it.

Whether we like it or not, we face toxic people and toxic situations throughout life. They are potentially one of the most unsettling and painful of occurrences. And they will leave us drained and demoralised if we allow them to.

That is why developing appropriate skills, competences and techniques will not only be extremely useful, but will also save hours and days (even months and years) of heartache and pain.

The seven Key Strategies have been developed to work in almost all situations and for every type of person. The toxic person could be a family member, work colleague, employee, boss, team member, friend or even a child. Sometimes they are just a person we are obliged to deal with every day. Equally, there are many stressful situations, but these learnings will be particularly useful when we are faced with people in administrative positions, such as government services, at airports, in public transport or call centres. Being forewarned and forearmed with the right know-how is to be prepared and confident when the need arises!

The most important first step in learning how to handle toxic people is, as we have made clear, to *get to know ourselves*. We must be aware of who we are and awake to how our ego and shadow operate. Knowing how we react and respond to toxicity and what our triggers are (which we explored and examined in Part 1) enables us to learn to master ourselves. From there, we can control our likely reactions *before* they come into effect.

Only by understanding and controlling our emotions and our reactions can we learn to effectively manage the toxicity of others. What we perceive in others and how we judge them is a reflection of our deeper, darker selves. Our 'perception' is really a *projection* of these unconscious thoughts and feelings. We unload them on to another to relieve ourselves of the guilt and shame associated with their being part of who we are.

The more clarity and understanding we have about our own deeper and repressed feelings, the better the prognosis for understanding and mastering our reactions—and hence managing those of others. When dealing with the toxicity of others, we are dealing with many of our own anxieties and stresses. We are facing our dislikes and disapprovals of our own being. We are similar in many ways to the toxic people we encounter. We are like brothers and sisters. And, in our judgments and pre-judgments, just as hypocritical.

The poet Baudelaire recognizes this in his poem '*Les Fleurs du Mal*' ('The Flowers of Evil') when he writes:

Tu le connais, lecteur, ce monster délicat,
— Hypocrite lecteur, — mon semblable,
— mon frère!

(You know him reader, this subtle monster,
— Hypocritical reader, — my mirror image,
— my brother!)

The author is calling attention to the way people are very quick to condemn and point the finger at others' 'sin'. While in private, they commit many of these same sins for their own pleasure and gratification—spurred by the same dark motivations and toxic thoughts. They—and we—are as guilty as everyone else. Understanding and recognising this is the beginning of compassion, forgiveness and redemption. It is the beginning of wisdom.

As we have already indicated in Part 1, the concept of *knowing thyself* is a fundamental life principle and has been reflected in almost all religions and philosophies for centuries.

Knowing who we are is the key to wisdom. It is also the foundation stone for mastering the most effective ways of managing toxicity and of avoiding the potentially catastrophic consequences of not doing so.

In *The Art of War* Sun Tzu says:

Know others and know thyself, and you will not be endangered by innumerable battles.

Sun Tzu stresses his firm conviction, based on experience, that by knowing ourselves and others deeply we can avoid very real dangers. The 'innumerable battles' we face today are our encounters with toxicity and dealing with toxic people. They can be deflected best when we know who we are and the nature of the other party.

Dealing with toxic people, therefore, requires a deep self-awareness and the ability to self-regulate when the need arises. This is what 'maturity' is generally about. However, the next step is one in which all of life is led authentically and naturally—without grasping, clinging or anxiety. In Zen Buddhism, this is called Wu Wei, meaning 'effortless', not in the sense of laziness but in the sense of tension free. We no longer need to force anything and work with nature and life's circumstances. We enjoy the process of living!

In this mental state of calm attention, events can be observed more objectively and without needing to label or prejudge. We become witnesses, creating a space for considered reflection. But to achieve this requires a profound understanding of how our ego and its shadow impact our thoughts, emotions and behaviours. Again, this is why the sections in Part 1 on ego, triggers and the shadow are so important for the execution of these strategies.

Mastering the self, when faced with a toxic person, means having:

a) the self-control to override the automatic kneejerk reaction of our own ego;
b) developing the virtue of patience to use time to carefully assess any toxic situation;
c) cultivating the discipline to remain silent when first confronting toxicity—since anything we say in the heat of the moment will be generated by ego and is unlikely to be helpful.

By practising these three consciously and regularly, we retain and build our power. This power allows us to be in a strong position to address any toxic person or situation. We will do so simply, patiently and compassionately.

> I have just three things to teach:
> simplicity, patience, compassion.
> These three are your greatest treasures.
>
> —Lao Tzu, Tao Te Ching,
> interpreted by Stephen Mitchell

We can practise them by consciously observing our own behaviour in everyday situations. When we are in a car, for example, and someone drives too close behind us showing impatience (and risking an accident) how do we react? Or if someone brushes past us aggressively while walking and nearly knocks us over? Or when someone sneakily slips into a parking space we have been patiently waiting for? It should be relatively easy to imagine many similar situations (which is also an essential part of the exercise).

We can then practise mastering our emotional and psychological responses by:

a) visualising ourselves being patient;

b) observing ourselves being compassionate (the other person's 'toxic' impatience may be due to reasonable circumstances and we may just be projecting our impatience on to them);

c) simply moving on. (Who cares? Does any of this really matter to us in the grand scheme of things?) Remember Wu Wei!

We should practise these techniques regularly. Then begin to increase the complexity and intensity of the situations we visualise. This will build our power to master ourselves and to be equipped when these situations occur in the world. Visualisation and repetition will create a new reality. They constitute a well tried and tested method for shifting perception and developing new habits.

Many of these skills can be categorized under the term emotional intelligence or EQ (emotional quotient). However, we are adding the all-important ability to separate ourselves from and become the witness of our egoic mind. By giving ourselves the time to rise above the personal internal struggles raging at the 'lower' level of ego, we will be in a much better position to see the very human interactions taking place.

If, however, we fail to rise above the turmoil, we will simply get dragged into it and become as 'unconscious' as the toxic person themselves. When our toxicity has been triggered, and we respond in kind, it is extremely difficult to escape. We fall down into a vicious cycle of tit-for-tat argument, which leads only to disappointment and suffering. Our only option if this happens is to *withdraw as soon as we can*—before things get even worse!

In Part 1, we examined aspects of the Self, in particular our behaviours and what drives them. Critical to the successful handling and management of any toxicity, however, is a deeper understanding of who the 'I' behind the behaviours actually is! Who are we really?

To begin to understand who we really are, we need to consider and dismiss who we are not:

a) Contrary to our likely first response, we are not our name! That is, after all, just what our parents decided to call us. It says nothing about who we actually are.

b) We are also not our thoughts. We *have* thoughts. Our mind generates many thousands of thoughts every day—about the past, the future and everything imaginable. But they are just randomly created thoughts. Since ego is the generator of many of these thoughts, we use them to create an identity. But an identity based on wishful thinking about who we are is just a fabrication and illusion—seductive but unreal. Thoughts reflect ideas, ambitions, dreams, fantasies, but they are not who we are.

c) We are not our job title either. Or all the roles we play. Or the responsibilities that have been given to us or we have assumed. These are just temporary activities that we have taken on. They are not who we are.

d) We are not our history, track record or CV. True, there may be things we have 'achieved' but they are all past events, figments of our imagination and history (and often very inaccurate and self-serving ones). Our 'history' is certainly an aspect of our life that has contributed to our personality and the identity we have chosen to assume. But our history is not truth. At best, it is only a fading, selective, memory trail of past events. One which we embellish and frequently enhance with imaginative exaggerations—not to say outright lies. Believing that our history is anything more than a memory trail results in our assuming a sense of self that is grossly overinflated. Human beings have a remarkable capacity for self-deception.

We will be aware of many public and private figures whose personal sense of self is totally unrealistic. They believe their own hype so much that they have been completely overcome by their ego.

Ego needs all these illusions to maintain its existence and identity. Without such illusions, the false sense of self, which we have lived with all these years, ceases to exist. If ego perishes—because the light of truth demolishes the illusion—then we, who are wholly invested in that illusion of self, perish too. This is often the result of a personal catastrophe or some other disaster.

Imagine you are someone others look up to, such as a top athlete, famous musician or even a spiritual teacher with disciples! Imagine you are recognized for your achievements. People admire you and you feel boosted by the praise you receive.

Over time, your ego takes over and conditions you to believe that *you* have achieved all this. It is you who are supremely gifted and that no one else could possibly have helped you. You begin to feel really 'special'.

Your ego will do all it can to perpetuate, even enhance, this illusion. It will then defend this image mercilessly if attacked. This defence could mean lying or being intolerant of others and their well-meaning advice.

Ego must absolutely defend the illusion for the simple reason that were an attack to succeed, your (false) identity would immediately be destroyed. If the image is who you think you truly are, and that image is destroyed, then you are also destroyed. It is a kind of living death.

Unless we realize that we are not these images, the effects of such disappointments are often catastrophic. There are many well-known cases of celebrities, notably retired sportspeople or pop stars who are no longer popular, who resort to more and more extreme means to get back into the public eye. Worse still, these people fall apart in desperation and resort to drink, drugs or even suicide. The same is true in other areas, when previously 'successful' people fail in their latest venture and the impact on them is disastrous.

However, it is not only the famous. We often hear stories of people who on reaching retirement find they have nothing to do and no purpose. Similarly, mothers suffer from depressive 'empty nest' syndrome—they feel they have finished being who they thought they were and now have no meaning to life.

We see the same thing all too frequently with young people. They believe that their body image does not match the (illusory and contrived) 'perfect' bodies they see on social media. As a result, they go into deep depression or develop other serious mental illnesses. They believe their 'I' should match the images they see. It is pure fiction and the work of ego. But they are only too willing to fall under ego's hypnotic spell.

These and other cases are the cause of so much depression, alcoholism, drug abuse, burn-out, heart attacks and even suicide.

Such disasters occur when a person becomes trapped in their egoic belief. They have attached themselves, often desperately, to an image ego has created, which is just a mirage. Ego creates a very addictive drug called 'me'—my image, my fame, my possessions… me, me, me—only it's all an illusion. It is not who they are. It is just thoughts and flights of fancy, which they have been fooled into believing are real. The image they are following is not who they are. Unfortunately, they cannot see it. The greater the illusion, the greater the ultimate fall and the more intense and acute the suffering.

Without being awake to the false sense of self created by ego the likelihood of our own ego being triggered by the toxicity of another is very high. We will then fail not only to manage the toxic person, but also our own toxicity. One ego will trigger the other—leading to a cycle of automatic unconscious and negative reactions.

Understanding that we are *not* the fabricated image of our ego is then an *essential first step* in understanding who we really are. If we persist in believing the illusionary images of who we think we should be, we will persist in egoic behaviour. This will make it impossible to manage either our toxicity or the toxicity of others. This is why we place so much emphasis on being self-aware and, most importantly, on being entirely comfortable with this truth.

So, who are we?

If we are not our name, our thoughts, our ego-image, our accomplishments, our title, our life story, then who are we at the deepest level? And how do we access this elusive 'I'?

First, let us come back to the millions of thoughts that swirl around in our mind with unceasing regularity. We have said we are not our thoughts, but how can we know this?

With a little effort, we can learn to observe our thoughts and become a witness to them. This means being consciously aware that these thoughts exist separately from ourselves.

When we are silent and quietly take the time to contemplate our thoughts, with practice we can decide which of these thoughts we wish to develop—and which to discard. We should observe without judgment, without attachment or tension and without being drawn into ego's game of compulsive repetitive thinking! Then we can learn to let go of those thoughts that do not serve us and adopt those thoughts that do.

In time, we recognize our thought patterns and the physical reactions to which they give rise. We can 'feel' the emotive internal reactions of our body *before* they manifest into responsive external action. With understanding and practice, we come to realize that it is actually quite easy to let go, because there is actually nothing to hold on to!

As we develop this emotional awareness, this 'awakening', we *create space* for common sense, also known as wisdom. We have already established that, since we are able to observe our thoughts, we cannot at the same time *be* those thoughts. The thoughts that we observe are now no longer controlled by ego, but by us. We have taken ownership back. We are the observer, the 'I', the witness, the presence that goes beyond thought and ego.

This is how we begin to learn to master ourselves and to regain our power. And what is more, we can do it easily and effortlessly: Wu Wei—the art of living without toxicity or stress, the art of doing nothing but accomplishing everything.

> The master does nothing, yet he leaves nothing undone.
> The ordinary man is always doing things, yet many more are left to be done.
>
> —Lao Tzu, Tao Te Ching,
> as rendered by Stephen Mitchell

Ego cannot co-exist with any of this and will work very hard to seek to fill the space we have created with anxieties about the past and concerns about the future. Ego's very existence depends on generating thoughts, most of which are designed to keep us in tension, expectation, envy and fear. Ego's 'job' is to protect us in the only way it knows, which is to make us fearful, based on our past conditioning. Ego needs fear to survive. That is how it works. It is always hovering around, looking to raise some anxiety or worry in our mind. It is well known that those who seek to control us use fear to do so. This method is attuned to the way our ego works. By preying on our anxieties, we are more likely to be persuaded and to comply. This is the essence of marketing as well as all propaganda!

The absence of fear—through the *recognition, acceptance and mastering* of fear—is ultimate freedom. When we realize that fear is ego generated and learn to let it go, we regain our true power. This is the power of freedom. It is the freedom to act spontaneously, without anger or any other of ego's negative emotions. With this power regained, there is nothing we cannot achieve.

> Man cannot possess anything as long as he fears death.
> But to him who does not fear it, everything belongs.
>
> —Leo Tolstoy, *War and Peace*

It is critical to realize that ego, like our shadow, will always be with us. We will not be able to rid ourselves of it. Those who try to do so risk becoming 'holier than thou' fanatics who seek an equally illusory perfection. But we can manage it once we know how.

As soon as we become the witness rather than the protagonist of our ego and its thoughts (and thus separate ourselves by allowing some objectivity), we create a new space, a space of awareness. This space of awareness is a place of peace. It is a place from which we can take wiser, more compassionate, kinder, and more effective decisions. This space is the best possible place from which to manage toxicity in all its forms, because we are no longer 'attached' to it.

Importantly, this space, this awareness, is also *who we are.* We expand on this idea in the rest of this chapter, while in the following one, on Key Strategy 3, we show how this knowledge can be used to stay calm and avoid reacting.

Whenever we feel that our body is becoming anxious or stressed and we sense toxicity, we need to allow our deeper self, our spacious awareness, to observe, accept and surrender to this feeling. By embracing it—fully, openly and completely—we expose it to the light. By this simple act of calm observation and acceptance, we will discover that the toxicity will lose its power to unsettle us, and it will disintegrate.

The very act of creating objectivity and space dissolves any attachment we might have to these negative emotions. Fighting or seeking to repress our emotions only serves to make them stronger. Observing, exposing, accepting, surrendering and embracing will allow us to handle any tension or toxicity and move on.

> All things become visible when they are exposed by the light, for everything that becomes visible is light.
>
> —Ephesians 5:13

People will do anything, no matter how absurd, in order to avoid facing their own souls. One does not become enlightened by imagining figures of light, but by making the darkness conscious.

—Carl Jung

What you resist, persists.

—Anonymous

To understand the difference between our ordinary everyday egoic self and our deeper self, we can compare ourselves to the ocean. The waves on the ocean are our everyday self, while the ocean in its entirety is our deeper self.

In our everyday existence, we are conditioned to believe that we are a unique 'wave' that is separate and different from all the other waves. We rise and ripple on the surface and encounter all manner of adventures and traumas—from storms to periods of calm and sunshine. The surface of the ocean is where the everyday joys, tragedies and surprises of life take place. One moment we are exhilarated, the next in despair, and so on. This ocean surface, our everyday world, is in constant flux and change. That is its nature.

However, the problem with this partial analysis is that it leads us to think that life is a series of random events and that we are just a separate and unconnected wave. In reality, *we are not separate* at all. This wave—what we call our everyday self—is not only connected to but inseparable from a power and energy that is beyond words and beyond compare. This power and energy is the ocean water in the analogy.

This energy has been recognized by physicists, theosophists and mystics the world over. It has been called the eternal light, universal intelligence, infinite energy and the love that passes all understanding. This universal truth is the source of all existence. It is the universe to which we are connected, which we create, and which is who we are.

In the words of Alan Watts:

> Bring me a wave separate from the ocean and I will show you a person separate from the universe.

We are not separate from the universe for the simple reason that we are an emanation and a manifestation of the universe. It is our natural state. This is conscious awareness, which is also 'divine'. It is, in the words of the medieval philosopher and theologian Meister Eckhart, 'the innermost of the human soul'.

Although we are a wave, our non-separation from the ocean means there is thus another, much deeper and more profound side to who we are. At this deeper level, in the quiet, still depths of the ocean itself, the activities on the surface seem insignificant, trivial and transient. From this shift in perspective, the daily tantrums of life become almost meaningless. They come and go but have little real impact. They are unreal in the sense that they are impermanent and constantly in flux.

> To a mind that is still, the whole universe surrenders.
>
> —Chuang Tzu,
> translated by Arthur Waley

What is real—what really matters—is our deeper self, our conscious awareness. It has substance, stability and permanence. This is the bedrock of our truth, the foundation of our moral stability. When we access this more profound, aware and present self, we find the key to handling any trial, tribulation or toxicity that appears on the surface. We have gone beyond our conditioned ego and transcended to a new level.

> The key to growth is the introduction of higher dimensions of consciousness into our awareness.
>
> —Pir Vilayat Khan

At this level, we do not need or have any desire to take ourselves so seriously. We know who we are and realize that human life is a gift, which is very short. *Life is meant to be lived.* We should make the most of it.

Once we recognize and accept that our deeper self exists *beyond* the trivialities of day-to-day events and *beyond* the illusions created by our egoic grasping, we access a place of peace and love. (This recognition should not be in a superior or smug way but with humility, compassion and understanding.) From this place of goodness—the ego-free, judgment-free state of pure presence—we are able to address the toxicity around us in a very different way.

We realize with great clarity that the solution to toxicity is never about being 'right' or 'wrong', about 'control' or 'submission', 'winning' or 'losing'. This duality of 'either-or' has no relevance in our reasoning. Having come through the doors of our new perception with new eyes, we seek understanding with compassion and find acceptable and wise solutions with kindness and consideration. We look to find gentle ways of showing appreciation, with respect for the dignity of others.

We take on board the necessity of taking full responsibility for our life and our actions. We cease looking for scapegoats. We wish to live an authentic life in which we are true to ourselves. We make mistakes, own up to them and learn from them. Who never makes a mistake never grows.

> The only man who never makes a mistake is the man who never does anything.
>
> —Theodore Roosevelt

Stripped of the grasping demands of ego, it becomes clear that we do not actually need anything—because everything is already within us.

> All you need is already within you, only you must approach yourself with reverence and love.
>
> —Nisargadatta Maharaj

> When there is no desire, all things are at peace.
>
> —Lao Tzu, Tao Te Ching,
> as interpreted by Stephen Mitchell

> When you realize there is nothing lacking, the whole world belongs to you.
>
> —Lao Tzu, Tao Te Ching,
> as interpreted by Stephen Mitchell

When it becomes clear to others that we seek no personal gain, we create an environment of trust. When they see we are only intent on discovering a way to peace, have put ourselves in their shoes and are looking for ways to help, then all things become possible. This is the *best place* from which to manage toxic people and toxic events. It gives the highest probability of a favourable outcome.

At the deepest level, we are particles of universal love and every aspect of the existence of life. Yet at the human level, we are just actors playing roles.

The words person and personality come from the Latin *persona* (and Greek *prosopon)* meaning a 'mask'. This derives from the Greek theatre, where different masks represented the various *personae* in the play. As we have said previously, there is a very similar idea in Hindu mythology. There the universe is likened to a drama in which human beings, who are manifestations of Brahman, the Absolute Self or God, enact roles and wear many masks. These illusions take them away from who they really are. They forget their divine origin and source and act in insane ways. GK Chesterton calls these personae 'the million masks of God'.

Hindu scripture suggests that all these masks are Brahman having fun! Sometimes they lose their way in an extreme manner until, eventually, sense is restored and the soul rediscovers its true source and spiritual identity. The more extreme the performance, therefore, the more the ego-obsessed individual actor loses touch with their real self. This makes their inevitable, ultimate and calamitous demise all the greater. This is acted out in the extravagant and colourful performances that are so popular in India.*

---

* Occasionally, I have congratulated (politely, calmly and without animosity) a toxic person acting disproportionately on their

Understanding and being comfortable with who we really are and accepting our failings and fallibilities openly and honestly are the foundation stone for successfully managing toxicity. This means always seeking truth—however difficult that at times may be—and connecting to conscious awareness and our natural, loving state.

'outstanding performance'. It has had the immediate effect of stopping them in their tracks! They are bewildered by such an unexpected comment and are puzzled about its meaning. Such a comment serves to stop the toxic person's line of thought—if only temporarily. When they then ask what I'm talking about, I have explained gently (without judgment or sarcasm) that I have been tremendously impressed with their impassioned performance worthy of the best actors. The way they have acted the part of an obnoxious, angry, toxic person in such an astonishingly realistic way has been magnificent and highly believable. I have then added that I can only assume this to be a role they are playing for effect, since it is obvious they are otherwise sincere, intelligent and kind human beings. In *most* cases, this has resulted in a marked reduction of tension, even laughter. This is purely anecdotal. I do not recommend that you try it at home! —Vernon Sankey

13

Key Strategy 3: Stay Calm, Do Not React

Be open, present and aware

With a deeper perspective of who we are and knowing how to access this place of relative calm, we are now in a position to come face to face with toxicity. This is where, as they say in the States, the rubber hits the road!

When we do find ourselves unavoidably confronted with an aggressive, obnoxious and toxic person, we need to use Key Strategy 3: *Do not react.* The primary instinctive response of ego would be to react (as we have shown in the previous chapters) but do not succumb! Instead, stay consciously 'in presence', with your wits about you. Stay in touch with your inner power and always, always, always stay calm.

Use *active listening skills* to show that you are interested in the other person's issue and avoid the temptation to interrupt. Allow them to say what they want and to get it off their chest. The aggressive, toxic person's ego needs continuous 'feeding'. This is especially so if they are angry, jealous, resentful, or feel neglected or belittled—sometimes all of these at the same time! Their ego needs to feel important, in control and 'right', especially when they feel under threat. They are drowning in an ocean of 'duality', meaning that they see everything in 'relative' terms: good/bad; happy/miserable; friend/foe; love/hate; win/lose. They see everything as either/or, and are unable to open themselves to both/and solutions. Because they are living in a purely competitive frame of mind, they find it very difficult to compromise, collaborate or seek a better solution. The toxic person's ego needs to be constantly acknowledged and reinforced and can never get enough conflict.

This toxicity is rarely seeking a genuine resolution to its many issues. To find resolution, you have to look critically inside, but to do so would be to deny ego. Rather ego is venting in order to justify itself. It is looking externally to find scapegoats, to blame others, blame 'circumstances', 'bad luck' or 'fate'. Ego complains of having been 'deceived' by others, been 'lied to', having inherited bad genes, bad parents, poor schooling. Ego blames pretty much anything except itself. The toxic person's life is being directed by their ego and its shadow. Until they are able to face and reconcile themselves with their dark side, their toxicity will resurface at regular intervals and dominate their psyche.

By simply being there, you become the focus of their egoistic inadequacies and their anger. They will project their self-loathing and pain on to you. Their ego will then attribute the cause of their problems to you—irrespective of the role you are playing. As far as their ego is concerned: anyone in the way is probably guilty! It is very easy to fall into this trap and react. You might either respond in kind—angrily and join the fight—or assume some element of responsibility and feel guilty or ashamed.

You are not responsible. You are not to blame. You are a victim of a toxic person's wrath and their fervent desire to pass on to you their desperately low self-esteem.

Stay calm, do not react and say nothing

Do not attempt to beat the toxic person at their own game. And do not allow yourself to fall into their trap. They have years of practice and will always win a battle fought on their territory. Do not seek to defend yourself—even against their completely unrealistic and outrageous arguments. Nor should you attempt to explain your actions, behaviour or feelings.

Defending is a reaction of your ego and will be viewed as an assumption and confession of your guilt. Your words will not only fall on deaf ears, but will indicate your willingness to join the fight—a fight we have already established you cannot win in this way.

Remember that *reacting* is an unconscious behaviour whereby we direct our energy *outwards into the world* to defend ourselves from an attack (or counterattack the other person). The result is an increase in tension and drama, the objective of which is to be vengeful and project blame on the other person. It does nothing to help resolve matters. It is our way of attempting to lessen or sedate the intensity of our own experience.

Responding, on the other hand, is a choice that we can make consciously. We control and manage our internal energy and confront our subconscious instincts, with a view to finding responsible and mature solutions. Sometimes our best response when confronted by toxicity is not only to control any desire to react, but to deliberately keep silent, while we think through carefully our best strategy.

By not reacting, by keeping cool and keeping an emotional distance, by saying nothing while the storm rages, we take the wind out of the sails of the other's ego. Ego cannot co-exist with silence.

In the absence of a response, it has nothing to push against. In its extreme discomfort, the other person's ego will try even harder to provoke. It will try to destabilise the situation and even sometimes threaten violence—'the last refuge of the incompetent', as Isaac Asimov so perceptively said.

By remaining quiet, however, the toxic person's rage will inevitably subside and blow itself out. This quiet should not come out of fear or feeling superior (which would be a reflection of our ego being triggered) but from a place of understanding, of genuine dignified listening. When this is regularly practised it is love. If the ego has nothing to push or fight against, it will be starved of energy and will stop fighting. Non-reaction, self-confident calm, observation without judgment are the best ways to handle such toxic attacks. No reaction means no fuel for ego.

It is important to remember when we are dealing with a toxic person that they are 'ill'. By this we mean, they do not know what they are doing. The famous words of Jesus on the cross express this perfectly:

> Forgive them, for they know not what they do.

They have no choice because they are completely under the control of their ego. And will remain so until their ego runs out of fuel. Until then they are totally at the mercy of their emotions, which they cannot control.

Toxic people are literally 'out of their mind'. Who, in their right mind, would consciously choose to suffer and to project such suffering, pain and distress? Instead of finding peace and creating happiness? It makes no sense. In this state, they are truly mad.

By managing our emotions, we defuse the toxic bomb. This means staying open, present and aware, and learning to stay calm. We also have to resist speaking, defending, judging, explaining or being triggered. It takes a little practice, but it is very effective.

We should try this out in small, less acute circumstances first. We will experience the significant and beneficial effect of this aspect of Wu Wei—of 'not doing'. We will not be grasping at solutions, not defending anything, not seeking to be right. Rather we will be just Being—open, present and aware.**

Studies have shown clearly that managing emotions in times of stress and remaining calm under pressure is what distinguishes the most effective performers in every walk of life. This is an essential quality of leadership. It engenders trust and builds confidence, and creates loyalty, enthusiasm, creativity and alignment. It is also a quality that keeps stress under control and promotes mental stability and health.

** I use this technique frequently in all sorts of circumstances and find that it is highly effective. (When it doesn't work, it's usually because I have allowed myself to be triggered and spoken too soon or said the wrong thing. In other words, some sort of judgment!) If I cannot avoid the toxic person or their toxic outburst, I wait patiently and with as little expression as possible—facially or bodily—so as not to express a judgmental, emotive reaction. When the 'rage' subsides, what often happens is that the other party will ask why I am not reacting at all (as their ego is utterly confused). I will then say: 'Because I know who you really are behind this drama and that this outburst, anger or suffering is not you, but a reflection of some genuine unhappiness, pain, resentment, problem, mishap or misunderstanding. I have great regard, admiration and love for you and would like to help, and, if it's me who you think has failed in any way, to make it right. So how can we resolve this together?' —Vernon Sankey

Our disciplined and quiet self-control is our best means of managing toxicity and of starting the process of handling any toxic person. This applies to one-on-one live communication, but works equally well with written communication. If the toxicity is expressed in writing (emails, messages, posts or blogs) the same holds true. Any response, if one is needed, should be delivered with calm, considered, polite dignity.

This never means accepting anything that is unacceptable or violates our principles. Nor does 'surrendering' mean 'giving up' or avoiding standing one's ground (see Key Strategy 4 on *establishing boundaries*). Sometimes, after the storm has abated, we do have to make our position clear. If we have something to say, we should concentrate on the facts only—devoid of emotion. Do not allow yourself to become 'unconscious' by matching the unkind, emotive comments of the toxic person, blow for blow. Be assertive (see Key Strategy 6) and clear. Stick to the truth and do not use emotional or provocative language.

After a period has elapsed, and once the toxic person has calmed down, it may be possible to explain your 'non-reaction'. However, this depends on the person, the nature of the relationship and the circumstances and has to always be done with genuine empathy. You can explain your unwillingness to be triggered, respond angrily or defend anything is because you love and respect them. You know who they really are—beneath the negative behaviour. You have seen and experienced their kind, gentle, generous side and you know that their outburst is a product of their ego seeking conflict, and not them. It is their behaviour that you dislike and find unacceptable and not them.

(Incidentally, this is also effective with children who misbehave. Never criticise the child, only their behaviour. That way the child does not feel fundamentally inadequate or diminished. They can turn their energy and focus on what they are able to work on, not on what's wrong with *them*. Then they can improve their behaviour.)

This discussion can only be achieved with authenticity, a high level of maturity and EQ and from a place of genuine love. Do not focus on negative behaviours but refer to those positive aspects of character that you have truly experienced. Do not gild the lily. Nor try to dampen the issue. It must be faced, honestly and compassionately, but in a straightforward way and without embarrassment.

While a valuable precursor to achieving a deeper and longer-lasting solution, such a discussion will not itself resolve the underlying fundamental problems from which this toxicity has arisen. This is likely to require a much deeper examination (perhaps also therapy from an experienced practitioner) to establish the true underlying causes. But it will provide a platform for addressing and managing the immediate toxicity from a calmer and more constructive position and for moving forward.

Up to this point, we have spoken of 'staying calm', but, as you know, this is not always easy. We now want to share a *practical exercise* that will help you to remain calm and stay in your peace—even in the most stressful of times.

It is a simple exercise to adjust our perspective from focusing on things and form, which we could call 'content' (and which will tend to be stressful) to focusing on space and formlessness, which we could call 'context' (and which will tend to be calming and ethereal).

We have found this practice very helpful and easy to do. Follow this guidance, whenever you need to de-stress and find or keep your calm:

i) Consciously observe, as you look around, what your eyes are focused on. Our eyes are conditioned to look at things. Our conscious minds shine a 'spotlight' on objects. The more stressed and anxious we are, the more our eyes will exhibit tension and the more we will concentrate our attention on things directly. We are focusing on content and form (to the exclusion of context and formless).

ii) Now allow your eyes to soften. Let them go slightly out of focus and shift your attention, your consciousness, from the objects in the room to the space around them. As you move from 'spotlight' to 'floodlight', tune in to the spaciousness of the room—the area that constitutes the greatest part of the room and that envelops you in its embrace. If you are outside, connect to the immensity of the sky and to unbounded nature.

iii) With your eyes soft, slow your breathing down and breathe deeply for a count of five.

iv) Allow yourself to sink into and bathe in this feeling of spaciousness, without any effort or stress. You will notice that all sense of 'you' and of ego gradually evaporates. All there is left is an 'oceanic' feeling of oneness and a sense of calm. You are connecting to the fullness of life, to the wholeness of being and to eternity.

v) This spaciousness, this sense of open, ego-free, awake presence, is who you really are. It is you without the trappings of things or thoughts or ego. You are not going anywhere, nor seeking anything. You just *are*. I AM.

To just *be*, without ego-driven obsessive attachment to anything, allows us to let go of any tension, suffering or of any illusions about self. Letting go of the concept of 'self', or of 'self' being different from 'other', is *Anatman*, or *Anatta*. These are the Hindu and Buddhist words meaning 'non-self'. If there is no self or ego, there is no lack. If there is nothing lacking, there is just (formless) peace and stillness. Everything we require is already here. We simply need to develop our ability to see it.

This practice very rapidly allows us to shift our perspective. We move simply and easily from the tensions associated with the content of life to the context of life, which is Life itself. We now have the key to open the door of our self-imposed prison and access the fullness and wholeness of existence.

This practice is a form of meditation but without resorting to anything complicated or difficult. As we apply it to our daily life and learn to become attuned to this consciousness and discover our inner peace and calm, we find that all the resources we need to deal with life's toxic challenges emerge more easily.

14

Key Strategy 4: Set Boundaries

Know what you can and cannot control

Right now, the only things we can control are our thoughts and our actions. Everything else lies outside our control—direct or even indirect. We can *try* to control through coercion, guile, diplomacy or persuasion. This may work for a short while, but we are still not able to control the outcomes. It can only be a short-term solution.

In the chaotic, ever-changing world in which we live, it is easy to feel frustrated, angry and powerless. This is particularly true of the tense, anxious situations caused by toxic people. This is a function of our desire for (and attachment to) certainty, security and clarity in an uncertain, insecure, opaque world. The more we try to control and strive after certainty, the more it will elude us. As a result, we become even more anxious and stressed. We are trying to do the impossible. Alan Watts describes this as 'trying to lift yourself off the ground with your own bootstraps'.

If it is futile to try to control others or the toxic situations we find ourselves in, what can we do? We come back to what we said at the start of this chapter: we *can* control *how we feel* about the situation that we are in. If we feel we are imprisoned, helpless, frustrated, those feelings are thoughts in our head. They are not real and are not true unless we permit them to be. The observation attributed to the Stoic Epictetus puts it well:

> Any person capable of angering you becomes your master; he can anger you only when you permit yourself to be disturbed by him.

If we do feel that we have the power to decide how we want to approach any given situation, especially a toxic one, this is also just a thought! Similarly, if we find alternatives and solutions with understanding and maturity or rise above the pettiness and anger, these too are thoughts. The difference is that these are thoughts that we can do something about! We can make them real because they are entirely within our control to do so.

> If you are distressed by anything external, the pain is not due to the thing itself, but to your estimate of it; and this you have the power to revoke at any moment.
>
> —Marcus Aurelius

Managing our 'self-talk' and *moving past negative thinking,* which only serves to send us into a negative spiral, is crucially important. While it is perfectly understandable to feel uncomfortable, unhappy or angry about a toxic situation or behaviour, negative self-talk will only make the situation worse. We will only dig deeper into our resentment and dream up increasingly aggressive scenarios of revenge.

Controlling our own thoughts and actions, especially when others are seeking to control ours, *is always entirely within our power*. It is key to handling such situations.

> If you really want to escape the things that harass you, what you're needing is not to be in a different place but to be a different person.
>
> —Seneca the Younger

If we learn to master our thoughts and actions, we are in control of much more than we sometimes appreciate. By controlling our thoughts, we create our own reality and our own universe. While we cannot and should not try to control other people, our mastery over ourselves will provide us with all the resources needed to take mature decisions. These decisions will influence any situation beneficially and enable us to better manage toxicity in all its forms.

Understanding we have power over our thoughts allows us to calmly make conscious decisions to establish the boundaries that will guide us—as well as the boundaries we wish to establish with others. Whatever the circumstances, it is up to us to carefully think through these boundaries first. We have to decide which ones we wish to establish with the toxic person. By setting, respecting and taking responsibility for these boundaries, we are not only exercising our power over ourselves but also over the outcome we wish to encourage.

The setting of our boundaries lies entirely in our hands. It is our responsibility and ours alone. If we fail to assume this responsibility, it is tantamount to handing over our power to someone else.

This never works and always ends in suffering. If we hand over our power to a toxic person, they will be only too pleased to take it! And they will use it against us.

Having made clear what we feel our boundaries should be, we need to express them, clearly and calmly, to the toxic party (see Key Strategy 5 on being assertive). If we believe those boundaries are being crossed, it is perfectly appropriate and essential to politely point this out and disengage and walk away. It may be that it is not the right occasion for a constructive discussion—for example, if emotions are running too high or there is insufficient time to find a considered, constructive solution.

Never be frightened to disengage. It is often the best decision, since to allow a boundary to be crossed sets a very bad precedent. Disengaging does not mean accepting the other's position. Nor does it mean that we are in any way 'surrendering' or weakly withdrawing. But it has to be done correctly. You can use the following steps, remembering to always act in a calm, controlled way:

i) Say that you are disengaging ('I'm not continuing with this conversation right now.')

ii) Say it straight—without anger, resentment or an attitude of superiority, inferiority, condescension or apology.

iii) If you feel the need to give any explanation, (and you really do not need to provide one) say you believe: 'It will be more sensible to stop and regroup at another time.' No other reason or explanation is warranted. The more you add, the more likely you are to be redrawn into the toxic morass.

We always have the right to set any limits we choose. Because, for example, we work closely with someone does not mean we have to accept their behaviour. We do not have to submit to unacceptable aggression or language anywhere—be it in the home, the office or online. The key to setting boundaries is to do this consciously and deliberately, with clarity about what they are and when they apply. In the workplace, it does not matter if what we are saying is already covered by law or company regulation. We should make no assumptions that a toxic person will abide by any regulation anyway—since the record shows that they do not!

By setting our own boundaries and explaining them clearly to the other party, we have the means to exercise important control over any situation—especially when the toxic person tries to destabilize the environment and cause dissention.

The absolute key is to hold to the boundaries we have established and not waver!

Once it is fully realized by the toxic person that your limits will be adhered to by you, it will be very difficult for them to argue against the boundaries. They are your prerogative to establish. It will also demonstrate your calm determination and strength. The toxic person (being a bully and, by definition a coward) will feel very uncomfortable but will have little to push back against.

However, if they do try to push back, *stay firm! A little persistence early on will save endless problems later.* Once established, an excellent precedent has been created from which you will also draw moral strength.

As with so many challenges, it is also important to choose our battles wisely. We need to learn when it makes sense to address an issue and when it is best to leave well alone. In the words of William Shakespeare's Sir John Falstaff in *Henry IV, Part 1*:

> The better part of valour is discretion.

When dealing with a toxic person, use time to think through the appropriate strategy. Step away if needed and do not get entangled. We generally have much more time to think things through than we imagine. We should use that time wisely. The toxic person will always be in a rush and will seek to 'bounce' us into an answer, an agreement or apology. Resist this pressure. Withdraw and take time to think things through.

For example, if we know someone (acquaintance, colleague or family member) who tends to be negative to the point of toxicity, we do not have to cut them off or never see them again. But we can decide *when and where* we wish to interact with them. With a more distant family member, it may be best to choose a neutral social setting. With a work colleague, it may be best in a location where there are other colleagues present. With an acquaintance, it may be best to limit the occasions in duration. Everything is possible—if we think through what is most appropriate first.

For a highly disruptive work colleague, we might set up a separate private meeting in a friendly location during which we go over some 'ground rules' (the boundaries). These boundaries would bind all team members and we would ask for their agreement to these rules. (And, if they do not like them, what can be done about them!)

Toxic people will frequently complain, blame and gossip negatively. They seek to drag their listener into their negative thought spiral. We should and can resist, if we have consciously established a boundary for ourselves that says we will not allow ourselves to be drawn into negative gossiping. It then becomes obvious what our position is. There is now no pressure to join in at all—either in support or in defence—however tempting this might be. We just do not engage in gossip and that is that!

Sometimes, we cannot avoid some form of engagement. For example, if we are a team leader who has an immediate need to restore a positive atmosphere in the group. A simple and effective way to achieve this is to ask how the toxic person thinks their complaint should be practically resolved and what *they themselves* would wish to do to solve them. This can then be debated by the whole group.

This solution has the effect of distinguishing between purely 'recreational' complaining and genuine problem solving. It also has the added benefit of moving the narrative away from emotions and towards greater rationality. In addition, it brings in the concept of responsibility. Complaining without taking responsibility for what can be done about it is entirely without value and a waste of people's time. The onus is thus placed on the toxic person to take responsibility for their complaint and its possible solution. Or to put it another way: 'to put up or shut up'.

15

Key Strategy 5: Be Assertive

Learn assertiveness skills, be sincere and use humour (carefully)

The skill of *assertiveness* is the oil that makes all the Key Strategies for managing toxic people work. For example, if we want to establish boundaries (Key Strategy 4), we have to communicate this in a way that will neither offend nor be dismissed. On the contrary, we want our communication to produce the desired result. This is an art that incorporates all the previous learnings on self-awareness, about 'who am I really,' and our ability to remain calm whatever the circumstances. It requires empathy and understanding of others. It also needs to be learnt.

Assertiveness is often misunderstood. It is frequently assumed that assertiveness means loud and pushy, verging on aggression, which it is not. Nor is it the opposite—passively accepting the views, opinions and decisions of others for the sake of a quiet life. Importantly, nor is it passive-aggressive when the more passive person appears to seemingly agree, when, in reality, they are seething inside. (Their resentment arises either because they feel ignored or belittled or because they suspect that others are exploiting their good nature.)

Assertiveness is our ability to *communicate clearly, openly, unambiguously.* We convey our meaning without embarrassment, while being conscious and sensitive to the position and needs of others and their responses. Communicating assertively includes the ability to express our feelings and beliefs as well as our personal rights. We voice our opinion even if this means disagreeing. We are prepared to defend a position and not allow another to take advantage of us. This skill is particularly important in these cases: with toxic people; when it is emotionally difficult; when we could lose something by doing so; or when establishing much needed boundaries.

When dealing with toxic people, being assertive means being prepared to state unashamedly how a particular behaviour makes us feel. It should not be in a way that accuses or blames directly, but rather explains the consequences that certain behaviours have on us.

When expressing how we feel, we should use 'I' statements, not 'you' statements. For example, 'I feel this way when you use this type of language' and not 'You always use bad language, which makes me angry.' This allows the other person to see the impact their actions are having without directly attacking them. Avoid the use of words such as 'always' or 'never', which are exaggerations and easily contradicted. The other person will then find the one occasion when they were 'right'.

All this said, there is no single, correct way to be assertive. Every person will develop their own style to suit their personality. Yet, whichever way we choose to express ourselves assertively, we need to develop these essential capabilities:

a) sufficient self-awareness and understanding of who we are to consciously recognize our feelings before we respond;

b) sufficient self-belief and understanding of our inner power to be willing to express our beliefs, ideas and thoughts clearly, without irony or emotional sabotage—especially when disagreeing with what is being said or done;

c) sufficient emotional self-control to be able to express different emotions (including desires, expectations and disapproval) in a consistent and coherent way;

d) sufficient empathy to be able to tune in to and be sensitive to the responses of others, adjusting the intensity level of our words and actions as necessary.

Assertiveness benefits significantly from absolute sincerity. Sincerity is not the same as seriousness, which implies a certain heaviness or dogmatism. Sincerity is lighter. It is more akin to authenticity, openness, the willingness to learn and to find win-win solutions. Being sincere means being completely honest about our feelings and our desire to express them in order to make things better.

Assertiveness is also enhanced by a sense of enthusiasm and positive encouragement. When dealing with a toxic person or situation, a quicker resolution will be found if we can say positive things about the toxic person and then offer constructive criticism (while also being prepared to listen carefully and receive it back).

In team situations, it can also be helpful to move to 'we' statements at the appropriate time. For example, when dealing with a difficult subordinate at work, who may be brilliant but is also sometimes disruptive and toxic, the objective will be to open a dialogue. You (as their boss) will explain calmly and clearly the impact their behaviour is having on you and why you feel a certain way when this behaviour occurs. Once the door is open, it is easier to move away from these 'I' statements to 'we' statements. The focus shifts to how the situation can be resolved to the benefit of the entire group and its harmony.

It is not necessary to expect the person to like what we are saying or to like us. Being assertive, especially in a business context, is not intended to win any popularity contests. But what is wanted is that the right message be honestly and sincerely received.

We want to promote the search for a lasting solution. The intention in this example is to retain a talented individual and their skills if possible. While, at the same time, clearly establishing the need to allow others to be brilliant too.

It should be firmly but calmly stated that teamwork and team cohesion are paramount. They enable collective brilliance to thrive and these values will not be compromised for the sake of any individual. It is important for this to be accepted first, before moving on. Once this is understood and accepted, it is possible to find constructive ways to improve the situation—for example, by providing coaching, different tasks, different teams or new job opportunities.

Assertiveness can also be made more effective when accompanied by humour. There is no doubt that a positive attitude to life and an enhancing sense of humour is a wonderful skill to have!

> Humour is the great thing, the saving thing after all. The minute it crops up, all our hardnesses yield, all our irritations and resentments flit away, and a sunny spirit takes its place.
>
> —Mark Twain

Studies have shown that having the right kind of humour improves mental and physical health, increases attractiveness and enhances leadership skills. It improves people's self-esteem, self-confidence, interpersonal relationships and overall quality of life, while reducing anxiety and stress. The phrase *laughter is the best medicine* has much truth to it. Laughter is known to reduce blood pressure, heart rate and muscular tension. A study from Northeastern University found that laughter lit up the anterior cingulate cortex, an area of the brain associated with attention and decision-making.

Humour can be a wonderful defuser of tension, bringing lightness to a dark atmosphere. *At the same time, humour has to be used with great care and emotional sensitivity.* Humour that is inappropriate or likely not to be found amusing by the toxic person (and toxic people tend to have a poor or very negative sense of humour) will actually make things worse. The use of humour is therefore a delicate matter. It can be a wonderful tension reducer but can also be a potential solution destroyer if done incorrectly.

There are many different theories about what humour is. Relief theory says it serves to reduce tension. The superiority theory (explained by Plato and Aristotle) argues we laugh at the misfortunes of others. Meanwhile, incongruity theory focuses on the unexpected, where clever wordsmithing, reversal or mingling of different ideas stimulate the imagination and make us laugh.

There are also different types of humour. Affiliative humour serves to strengthen relationships. Self-enhancing humour reflects a positive attitude to life and helps initiate team cohesion. While aggressive humour (including sarcasm and hostility) is where other people are mocked. Whereas self-deprecating or self-defeating humour makes the individual the target of their own jokes.

Most types of humour have their role to play, but they all require a high level of emotional intelligence if they are to be used effectively. However, we strongly warn against using negative, aggressive humour—especially with toxic people. Unless you are very expert at sensing when it might be appropriate, we would not recommend using sarcastic, demeaning humour any time. Making fun of others is not good practice!

Research has found that people who have a positive style of humour are generally better at forming good relationships and encouraging self-disclosure. While people with a predominantly negative sense of humour have less effective interpersonal skills, are less adept at managing conflicts or providing emotional support. They are less assertive, in the correct sense of the word.

Humour is a very valuable life skill that can enhance our ability to influence and improve many situations. However, as we have noted, it has to be applied with great care. If in doubt, do not use it! Keep to straight, honest, uncluttered facts and emotions.

As we have outlined, true assertiveness has many benefits. This becomes even clearer when we look at the alternatives:

a) *Passivity* is not helpful because it tends to foster resentment. The passive person is unclear, ambiguous or misleading in their expression. This leads to feelings of being ignored or belittled because acquiescence is taken as agreement when it is anything but. This culminates in misunderstanding and unhappiness.

b) *Passive-aggression* is the next stage of passivity. The passive person harbours negative feelings about any exchange. These feelings are bottled up for so long that when they explode they can be totally out of proportion to the event itself.

c) *Aggression* can never succeed for long and is both exhausting and self-defeating. It is a very unpleasant state of mind that sends out negative vibrations and attracts like-minded, equally negative responses. Studies have shown that angry, hostile, aggressiveness in people creates a higher risk of heart attacks than stress, cholesterol and other factors.

Compared to these negative approaches, assertiveness is a form of freedom and is highly liberating. It enables the assertive person to address difficult issues or people in a calm, honest, straightforward way. They can maintain their integrity and equanimity, even in difficult circumstances.

> When force of circumstance upsets your equanimity, lose no time in recovering your self-control, and do not remain out of tune longer than you can help. Habitual recurrence to the harmony will increase your mastery of it.
>
> —Marcus Aurelius

Being assertive not only allows difficult situations to be addressed unambiguously, but also shows respect for the other person.

In an assertive exchange, there is no aggression involved, no anger and no put-downs.

Assertiveness needs to be exercised, however, with care. Use eye contact, body language, tone of voice and choice of words with due sensitivity to the feelings and reactions of others. Assertiveness is a major key to managing toxic people and toxic situations.

16

Key Strategy 6: Focus on Solutions

What we focus on determines the outcome we seek:

> Energy flows where attention goes.
>
> —Tony Robbins

This idea has been around for a long time, and it has long been accepted that our present thoughts determine our future. There is a Buddhist quote that encapsulates this:

> What you think, you become.
> What you feel, you attract.
> What you imagine, you create.

If we use the present moment to fixate on past toxic events or future potential difficulties, our mind becomes overwhelmed with negative thoughts. These intensify our feelings of anxiety and disempower us.

If we allow our mind to be filled with images of how unbalanced, unreasonable and difficult the toxic person is (and how anxious and frightened we are about managing them), then we are handing over our power to them. We are filling our thoughts with *their* poison. And we are doing this blindly. The toxic person—or rather the image we have of them—has control over us and over our emotions. And this is even before any communication has taken place! In such circumstances, we will not succeed in managing the situation properly.

We can, however, shift our mindset from a 'victim' mentality to a 'victor' mentality. This happens when we fill our present thoughts with possibilities for us and alternative solutions that will work for both parties. This could be by considering how best to handle a toxic person, for example, rehearsing what we are going to say and how we are going to say it. It might be what boundaries we wish to establish or what solutions we can propose. Each time, we are actively promoting and nurturing our power.

By focusing on positive, solution-based possibilities, we are re-establishing control over ourselves and our emotions. At the same time, we are reducing stress. This is part of *active acceptance*, which means accepting that there is an issue to address *and* that we can face it positively, honestly and constructively—from a position of peace and truth. Thinking about win-win solutions and establishing a clear strategy for communicating assertively, lifts our mind out of fear mode and into positive action mode. It takes us beyond the heaviness of problems and into the lighter realm of possibilities and resolutions.

We are now doing the best we can with the best of motives. This builds our sense of self-confidence and self-worth. Furthermore, a positive solutions-driven attitude stimulates creative ideas for win-win solutions. However difficult it may be, the toxic person should also be encouraged to contribute to this process. Ask them to come up with alternative solutions—such as, 'How do *you* think we can best resolve this matter?' This will encourage them to begin to shift their mindset from negative to constructive thinking. By focusing on possibilities going forward, which we can influence, and away from the problems of the past, which we cannot, we are setting a framework to find amicable, workable solutions.

If, in spite of our best efforts, the toxic person chooses not to respond and insists on remaining uncooperative and negative, it is best to recognize this early and withdraw. Pushing at a locked door will not serve to open it! Having done our best, we can take comfort in the knowledge that we have acted correctly and compassionately. We may not have resolved the issue this time, but we have been authentic and positive. Tomorrow is another day.

Even though our self-confidence may have been somewhat dented, our self-regard—our honest knowledge of our strengths and weaknesses and respect for who we are—remains solid. From this foundation, we can regroup for another day or withdraw altogether.

By never allowing another to take our power away from us, we are free to decide the implications for us going forward. It may not be emotionally pleasant, but by keeping to our principles and values, we uphold our integrity and sense of self-worth. This is what freedom of choice means. By being positive and looking for solutions rather than seeking to win the argument or attributing blame, we are breaking the cycle of negativity—both in ourselves and with the other party—and opening the door to better possibilities.

The next stage of our freedom is for us to recognize the need to take full responsibility for our own future and for any decisions we take along the way. We are wholly responsible for our life and actions. Nobody else is. And nobody else should be held accountable for our current life and its predicaments. When we blame others, we give our power away. When we take responsibility, we take back our power and transform our life.

Liberty means responsibility. That is why most men dread it.

—George Bernard Shaw,
|*Man and Superman*

Freedom is the will to be responsible for ourselves.

—Friedrich Nietzsche,
Twilight of the Idols

Not all situations are capable of being rescued! With the best will in the world, not everything can be made right. It will only cause immense and continuous suffering to try to repair what is irretrievably broken. That is also part of life. We have to recognize this. Some issues are too difficult and painful to address. And sometimes, it just is not meant to be.

When this happens, we should learn all we can from the experience and move on. We should not make the toxic person's problems our problems—even if this is emotionally distressing in the short term. Everyone is on their unique journey of life and maybe this journey is the best one for them.

We can wave them off on their life with love and compassion so that we can move on. We will be creating a space for healthier and more wholesome future relationships. Having exhausted the search for solutions, we draw the matter to a final close.

17

Key Strategy 7: Build Great Relationships

Our last Key Strategy may seem obvious, but it is crucially important when dealing with toxic people and toxic situations.

Building great relationships has many benefits. They provide a support network of people who can be trusted to be with us when we need them most. At the same time, they constitute an invaluable and reliable source of honest, selfless advice in times of need. Our self-worth, sanity and overall wellbeing are enhanced by having around us friends and family who we know care for us and love us.

Great relationships enable us to spend less energy on the negative aspects of life and more time on ego-free and more relaxed, open, constructive exchanges. In times of toxic difficulties, being able to escape from the turmoil and find ways to enjoy life is immensely relieving.

Being in a toxic situation or relationship can easily make us feel isolated or alone. This damages our mental and physical health, increases cortisol levels and disrupts sleep. Studies have shown that good relationships lower rates of anxiety and depression, strengthen the immune system, increase self-regard and empathy, and inspire a greater level of belief in positive outcomes. It makes us more optimistic, which leads us to be more creative in finding suitable solutions. Having good relationships with family and trusted friends also helps make life safer. We can call on friends if circumstances descend into violence.

The ability to be open about difficult issues with trusted friends makes it easier to take a more balanced view. When we bring objectivity into the picture, it helps us to look at alternative action and maintain rationality when we doubt. It also diminishes anxiety and fear when we are at a particularly vulnerable time.

> A problem shared is a problem halved.
>
> —Proverb

> Friendship improves happiness and abates misery by doubling our joys and dividing our grief.
>
> —Cicero

However introverted or extroverted we might be, human beings are social creatures. We thrive and, in many respects, depend on our connections to others. We are connected not only to each other but to the whole of nature and the universe, without which we cannot exist. It is precisely when we develop and enjoy great relationships that we experience this wonderful sense of connection to a universal intelligence, an infinite light. We sense a divine power that is much greater than ourselves and that uplifts us.

> Keep holy company.... The companionship of the holy and the wise is one of the main elements of spiritual progress.
>
> —Sri Ramakrishna

> If the joys of heaven and salvation could be weighed together in a balance, they would not equal the happiness that results from a moment of *Satsanga* [holy company].
>
> —Sri Ramakrishna

> If you go off into a far, far forest and get very quiet, you'll come to understand that you're connected with everything.
>
> —Alan Watts

Toxic people believe themselves to be separate and act as bodies unconnected to anyone or anything else. Because of this sense of separation, they are selfish, uncaring and insensitive. They have lost their connection to any greater power and their morals with it. They believe themselves to be that greater power! This ego-driven illusion is ultimately disastrous for themselves—there is no way out of this narcissistic prison—but also catastrophic for those who are dragged into their web. Having people around us who can help to rescue us from this quicksand and bring us back to a safer place is vital.

Building great relationships is easier said than done. In addition, the fact that we have been caught in a toxic relationship points to opportunities for reflection on our own relationship-building skills. While there are ideas and pointers throughout this book that provide guidance on how to develop close, open and loving relationships (see also *The Stairway to Happiness*, *The Way: Finding Peace in Turbulent Times* and *The Way Workbook*), we have brought together seven principles here:

i) Know who we are, in all honesty and humility, and accept ourselves with all our strengths and our weaknesses. Doing the homework here allows us to observe our ego and control our emotions, be humble and authentic and understand that we are all connected to each other in absolute love, which is oneness. This will enable us to be open, aware and present in all our dealings.

ii) Develop our emotional intelligence, with particular reference to self-awareness, interpersonal skills, assertiveness, empathy, flexibility and optimism. Optimism enables us to send positive vibrations into the world and uplifts spirits. Smiling is the body's manifestation of optimism.

iii) Develop excellent listening skills: seek always to understand first and be understood second. Giving people your time by actively listening to them, by being truly present, is indeed a huge present that enriches any relationship.

iv) Develop excellent communication skills. This means saying what we need to say clearly and sympathetically. However, communication excellence does not finish when we have said something. That is just the start. Communication is only complete when we have checked that the person understands what we have said and has had the opportunity to respond. Communication is always two-way.

v) Learn to trust and be trusted. If we want to develop our trust of others, we have to learn to trust ourselves. This takes us back to emotional intelligence (ii) and the knowledge and acceptance of who we are (i). No love can last without trust and respect. Nothing can be built that is greater than the level of trust on which it is founded. If we want to be trusted, we have to be trustworthy. We need to open our heart and find the courage to trust.

vi) Learn to create an atmosphere in which people feel psychologically safe and able to raise and discuss issues in confidence. Create a space in which they will be respected for their views—whatever they are.

vii) Create a community of like-minded people who share the same values, seek common ground and look to cooperate and collaborate in an ego-free setting. When two or more people establish such a connection (from a place of acceptance and surrender) a state of magic is created. This magical state arises when people operate from consciousness and not compulsion, from truth and not ego, and from absolute love, which has no opposite.

We are all different and yet we are all connected to the same universal intelligence. We all have a right to be treated with respect and love. And we have a duty to do the same to our fellow creatures, living on the same planet. This golden rule, which is a feature of almost every religion and philosophy, is very sound and will do much to help us create wonderful, life-long relationships. If a few of our relationships develop into true friendships, then we are doubly fortunate.

> The glory of friendship is not the outstretched hand, not the kindly smile, nor the joy of companionship; it is the

spiritual inspiration that comes to one when you discover that someone else believes in you and is willing to trust you with a friendship.

—Attributed to Ralph Waldo Emerson

Don't walk behind me; I may not lead.
Don't walk in front of me; I may not follow.
Just walk beside me and be my friend.

—Anonymous

PART 3

Common Toxic Types: How to Apply the Key Strategies in Everyday Life

18

Introduction to Common Toxic Types

In this part, we show how the Key Strategies can be put into practice in identifiable situations. We have focused on four generic toxic characteristics and explain which of the Key Strategies (usually in combination) is most effective for each type.

You will notice that we recommend employing multiple Key Strategies and that the same strategies work, even though the exact toxic circumstances may be different. This is because the Key Strategies are robust and address the root causes across many toxic traits. The various examples are designed to help demonstrate their use under different circumstances and confirm their value.

We follow these generic types by getting even more specific with real-life case studies in Part 4. We explore what happened, what were the consequences and what might have been the outcome if different Key Strategies had been adopted.

Common toxic types

As we described in Part 1, when we are in the presence of toxic people, we immediately sense it. We pick up negative vibrations, feel uncomfortable and feel tension. This tension is our ego picking up the negative signal of the other person's ego and being activated. Our instinct, stimulated by our ego, picks up signals well before the mind has had time to process them or try to rationalize them.

As we learn and understand better who we are, we also learn to trust these signals. They arise in the body, triggered by the most primitive part of our subconscious mind that is designed to keep us safe. It picks up the subtlest of signals and activates our bodily response, including fight or flight. These signals include the low-level, rather dark, vibrations emitted by the toxic person—often accompanied by negative body language, aggressive tone of voice and tense facial expression.

Beyond the general sense of negativity, however, toxic people do also display certain groups of traits. It is extremely helpful to recognize and identify their specific thought processes, behaviours and actions as soon as possible. This allows us to be awake to what is likely to happen next and be better prepared to manage them.

We have identified four general toxic types. By recognizing the type and applying the relevant Key Strategies, we are in the best possible place when we do encounter a toxic person or situation.

Cynically negative

These individuals have a negative, often cynical worldview (which also extends to the company or their relationship). They expect and look for the worst. They rarely show enthusiasm or excitement. Even when faced with good news, they will put a negative slant on it. They are rarely impressed or in awe of anything and lack genuine enthusiasm.

Ungrateful and mean

They rarely recognize the contributions of others and are rarely grateful. They are not generous with their time or their money. They are mean minded.

Responsibility averse

These people avoid taking responsibility for their actions, preferring to blame and accuse others. When things go wrong, they believe themselves to be the hapless victims of other people's bad intentions or deliberate mistakes or of plain bad luck. They dislike taking decisions and deny responsibility for negative outcomes. They are poor leaders and tend to underachieve their potential.

Interpersonally flawed, hypersensitive and humourless

This type have frequent interpersonal issues and lose or discard friends easily. They have few real friends. They rarely show affection or warmth. They are frequently disrespectful, dismissive and harsh. They are also often angry for no apparently logical reason and lash out easily. They are hypersensitive, especially to criticism. Their inconsistent moods force those around them to feel that they are permanently walking on eggshells. They wear many masks—depending on what they want and who they are with. They find it hard to trust and are often secretive. Everyone and everything is suspect! They are often described as 'difficult' and are hard to live with. Their relationships are problematic.

The following four chapters deal with each of these types in turn. We show how to use the Key Strategies to effectively respond to their characteristics and be free of their toxicity.

19

Cynically Negative

How to use the Key Strategies to respond

Cynically negative people, as team members, colleagues or as a boss, are highly disruptive. They can demotivate and dishearten even the most positive and contributory people and teams. Negative low-level vibrations immediately dampen the atmosphere in the room, creating a depressive, sinking feeling. This destroys the enthusiasm, creativity and cooperative teamworking that thrives on psychological 'safety' and an open, constructive, listening environment.

People who lack enthusiasm and a sense of awe and are never demonstrably impressed with what others achieve most likely received little encouragement, support or recognition for their efforts during their formative years. Their parents, teachers and other 'authority' figures were probably critical and disparaging of their efforts. This repressed the natural instinct to celebrate and praise.

Because nothing was ever 'good enough' in their early life, they have grown up to expect that things will not turn out well. They will also be fearful of being blamed or taking responsibility. This leads to a preference for complaining and blaming when things do, inevitably, sometimes go wrong. Any setback becomes a validation of their pessimism.

The best Key Strategies for dealing with cynically negative people

The best Key Strategies for dealing with cynically negative people are **3**, **5**, and **6**.

i) First, apply *Key Strategy 3: stay calm and do not react* to the negativity. Do not fight or reject it (which is ego being triggered) or, even worse, for the sake of peace, placate it! Appeasing bullies does not work. Giving way in this manner simply encourages further bad behaviour. Be awake to the negative vibrations but do not rise to them. This does require maturity and a decent level of self-awareness and self-control but is essential.

ii) Then, apply *Key Strategy 5*, which is to ensure that any response you make, you do it *assertively*. Without aggression or embarrassment, keep to facts only and avoid emotions.

Whether this is a business meeting or a personal domestic exchange, the focus should turn to a genuine understanding of the negative person's point of view. (This is irrespective of whether or not there is justification for the negativity, such as a project not being on time, creative ideas inadequately generated, a domestic issue that is not realistic.) Do this by using calm assertive language to ask *open* questions.

iii) Negative comments that are gratuitous and unspecific should be addressed calmly, using *Key Strategy 6: focus on solutions.* Once again, do not engage with the negative emotions: focus on finding solutions to whatever issues have been raised. Bring in the negative person and insist that they contribute to the solution generation. If they are critical, they should take some responsibility for finding a solution. Do not allow them to get off the hook! In other words, and in the nicest possible way, encourage them to 'put up or shut up'!

20

Ungrateful and Mean

How to use the Key Strategies to respond

People who are ungrateful and mean-minded have a scarcity and fear mentality—rather than one based on abundance and love. They may well have grown up in an environment where they were rarely praised (and frequently criticized) and one in which every penny mattered. Expressions such as 'money doesn't grow on trees' prevailed and such images have stayed with them.

With regard to gratitude, their ego is fearful that if they praise other people for good work done, this will diminish how they themselves are perceived. As if, by giving due credit to others, this will reflect poorly on them. Their ego has created an identity that implies that the only good things that ever happen are a result of their own efforts and prowess. Showing gratitude to others then becomes a symbol of their inadequacy.

This perverse bravado covers up deep feelings of insecurity and a lack of self-confidence. Lacking trust in themselves, they find trusting others difficult.

When people do them favours, they may see this as something to which they are entitled. There is no need to be grateful. Although they are very sensitive to slights or criticisms, they lack the sensitivity to appreciate the significant motivational value of showing gratitude to others.

Ungrateful people tend also to lack generosity. Generosity is closely linked to gratitude. When we feel grateful for what we have, we are more willing to share our good fortune with others and be generous. Gratitude and generosity recognize that we are all ultimately interdependent and interconnected and that we never actually 'own' anything.

If we see ourselves as separate, however, and fighting a lonely battle for survival, then we will be protective rather than expansive with what we temporarily have. Ungenerous people will focus more on the cost of things (and what they might lose) than on their human value. People matter so much more than the cost of the generosity offered but they do not see it that way.

Being unwilling to 'give' applies to objects (money and gifts), but, even more importantly, it applies to human emotions such as affection, warmth and love. If we are ungenerous with our love, for fear of losing it and being hurt, we create for ourselves a lonely, emotional prison. We deprive ourselves of the most essential element of life and living. Regrettably, this is often the reality for the toxic person.

And when it comes to the workplace, lack of gratitude and generosity will be seen as egoism and selfishness. It will rapidly create resentment within any team.

The best Key Strategies for dealing with the ungrateful and mean

The best Key Strategies to deal with ungrateful and mean people are **1**, **2**, **4** and **5**. We will look at how to use them in both a personal and then a business context.

In an everyday, *personal context,* first employ *Key Strategy 1: recognize and avoid* becoming emotionally entangled with this form of toxic person. Try to *keep your distance* or it can become very expensive—emotionally and financially.

When the well-meaning, generous person meets someone who seems otherwise normal but appears to be rather ungrateful and mean, they will initially be puzzled by this. As long as they are not emotionally involved with the person, it will be relatively easy to walk away or limit contact. But if they become emotionally involved, their incomprehension regarding the lack of positive reaction may turn into self-criticism. They will be tempted to say to themselves: 'Perhaps I'm not doing enough?'

In their desire to please, they may then redouble their efforts. However, this will be in vain as the toxic person will continue to manipulate them.

In such cases, it is best to apply *Key Strategy 5, being assertive*, and then, if necessary *Key Strategy 4, setting boundaries.*

However painful it may be, it is crucial to bring the matter into the open and address it calmly. While this may result in disagreement, it is preferrable to being in a constant state of anxiety and unhappiness because we do not understand what the problem is. When addressing the matter, we should not criticise the other party but rather explain how we feel when we receive no responses to our kindnesses. The response we receive back will be highly indicative of the state of mind of the other party and of the relationship.

For the best chance of success, however, we should *know who we really are*—a central part of *Key Strategy 2*. Understanding who we are, in all honesty and humility, means being comfortable with our strengths and weaknesses and authentic in all our dealings. This gives us an unassailable platform of goodness and strength. From this place of calm and peace, we can be properly assertive (Key Strategy 5) and the likely outcome more acceptable and positive.

In a *business context*, ungrateful and ungenerous people make very poor leaders. Their inability or unwillingness to recognize the efforts of others or be generous with their time ('management by wandering around' can be critical) will create an environment of uncertainty and mistrust in the leadership. Underperformance will result. When people feel they are being taken for granted and coerced rather than encouraged, they rapidly become demotivated and resentful. And the best employees will leave.

The supervisor/boss of such a toxic person should immediately address the issue openly and clearly (*Key Strategy 5, being assertive*). They should explain the negative impact created by behaviours that fail to recognize the successes and work of others. They need to make clear the vital importance of gratitude and generosity in creating a motivating climate of psychological safety, cooperation and collaboration. These are basic leadership skills that companies need to instil in all leadership positions.

21

Responsibility Averse

How to use the Key Strategies to respond

One of the most frustrating and irritating aspects of toxic people is that they are often incapable of taking personal accountability for decisions or their consequences. They will encourage others to take decisions on their behalf, but it becomes apparent that this is *not* to share the decision-making process. Rather, they are (very manipulatively) hoping to claim credit if things go well. And conversely, attribute blame and find fault with others should things go wrong.

One of the principal reasons they are frightened of taking a decision is because they lack self-confidence and wish always to be above reproach. They cannot accept that they might be seen to make a mistake. They have never learnt that it is only by trial and error that we learn, grow and develop. If we are conditioned in childhood to fear making mistakes, being wrong or being laughed at for our errors, our ability to learn will be curtailed. And we will be forever in conflict with ourselves—never able to be whole.

People who find it hard to accept accountability for their actions lack self-confidence and harbour deep doubts about themselves. Caught up in an ego identity that can never be wrong, they lack trust—in themselves and those around them. They are then perceived as unreliable and selfish.

In a business context, they will create disharmony and suspicion. They make poor team players, as well as uninspiring and demotivating leaders.

The best Key Strategies for dealing with the responsibility averse

The best Key Strategies for dealing with the responsibility averse are **1**, **4**, **5** and **6**.

It is important to detect this trait as soon as possible since it can be highly disruptive to any inter-personal relationship and, in the business context, to team cohesion, harmony and motivation.

In a *personal context*, use *Key Strategy 1, keep your distance,* if you can. This trait can be very disconcerting. The unfortunate victim of this type of toxicity can be led down a path of continuous anxiety if they allow themselves to fall into the trap of being the person who becomes the fall guy when things go wrong but remains unrecognized when things go well.

If we are already witnessing this behaviour and feel the toxic person could be receptive, we can speak to them using *Key Strategy 5, being assertive*. We will need to employ tact and sensitivity while being unambiguous and firm. The goal is to explain (perhaps citing personal examples) why making mistakes is normal and why accepting responsibility is a sign of strength and not weakness. (If you are a competent therapist or coach and the person shows a genuine desire to learn, then judicious counselling may be very beneficial.)

In a *business context*, if you are the supervisor of such a person, address this issue openly using *Key Strategy 5, being assertive*—that is, with sincerity and without embarrassment or aggression. You will be doing your employee a great favour if you can effect a change of a behaviour that would otherwise rapidly become career limiting for them. It is also your duty as a leader to help develop those in your care.

Explain why and how this behaviour—the inability to make decisions and take accountability for them, as well as blaming others when things go wrong—is highly detrimental to team harmony. Use specific examples to demonstrate the issue and illustrate its effect on others. It cannot be tolerated in a high-performing team. Encourage change by reinforcing the fact that we all make mistakes. Mistakes, and the vulnerability associated with them, are normal human occurrences and the best way to learn. Taking responsibility and accepting the consequences is what self-confident leaders do. By making themselves an example, they create an environment in which creativity and idea generation will flourish, as well as one where leadership is trusted and respected. Teams thrive when they feel safe, where there is genuine mutual support, when decisions are made openly and members are fully accountable.

In both personal and business contexts, if you are coaching a toxic person to help them to overcome this trait, it is important not to let them off the hook. Do not go along with the negative blame and gossip game or dilute the need for full accountability. This will do nothing to remedy the situation and will certainly not serve the person at all.

If we are involved (in any context) in the establishment of joint plans, we should follow *Key Strategy 6, focus on solutions.*

Emphasize the need for unambiguous decisions and their implications. Include clear accountabilities and responsibilities and what they mean in terms of individual and collective expectations and commitments. In this respect, you are also *setting boundaries* (*Key Strategy 4*) that are well communicated and understood.

When things turn out well, be sure to praise and congratulate. Do so openly and sensitively, leaving no one out. If things turn out unsuccessfully, be honest about accepting responsibility. Do not look for or tolerate excuses but rather focus on lessons that can be learnt for the future.

Learning to take responsibility for our decisions and our actions is the key to taking control and responsibility for our life. We shift from being a 'victim' of circumstances to being a 'victor'. We regain and strengthen our power. When we are unafraid of taking decisions and accepting accountability, not only do we learn more rapidly, but we discover a new sense of freedom to try things out. This further enhances the learning cycle and adds excitement to life. We can only find our calm and inner peace when we learn to accept that life is constantly in a state of change. We cannot control outcomes, only our own thoughts and our own decisions and actions. We are alive precisely because the one thing we can control is our actions. Being wholly responsible for them is an essential part of our aliveness.

22

Interpersonally Flawed, Hypersensitive and Humourless

How to use the Key Strategies to respond

People who are hypersensitive, often angry, disrespectful and inconsistent in their moods can be very distressing and disconcerting. Their serious inter-personal flaws make it very difficult to know what mood they are going to be in—and how carefully to tread. They drain the positive energies of others while seeking to feed their own ego.

It is likely that such behaviours will have been habitual for a long time. They usually arise from childhood as the after-effects of being neglected and ignored or (at the other extreme) pampered and spoiled. These people have an overactive ego and assume that their mood and sensitivities are more important than those of others. This is the selfishness and inconsideration of ego made manifest. It is often a cry for attention—even if that attention is a negative one. The premise is that it is better to get negative attention than none at all!

This behaviour shows a lack of empathy, self-awareness and self-discipline. They lack compassion and love for others (as well as for themselves) and their inter-personal skills are seriously flawed. Because they lack inter-personal skills and sensitivity to others' feelings, they will tend to be brusque and overly direct. They generally have a distinct capacity to bully others. Their sense of humour is often weak (or missing) and largely cynical because they see life through a negative lens. The amusing side of life escapes them. Everything is shrouded in clouds of heaviness and seriousness.

The best Key Strategies for dealing with the interpersonally flawed, hypersensitive and humourless

The best Key Strategies for dealing with the interpersonally flawed, hypersensitive and humourless are **1**, **2**, **3**, **5** and **6**.

If you have encountered such people, you will know they are difficult to live with. They make for difficult and rather stressful friends, and equally difficult-to-manage executives and team colleagues.

The main initial advice will always be *Key Strategy 1, avoid*, if at all possible. Keeping a distance from such people will avoid future pain and disappointment. If occasional contact is inevitable, then do not allow yourself to be drawn in (also part of Key Strategy 1!).

If more frequent contact is inevitable, then it is vital to adopt *Key Strategy 3, remain calm* at all times. Stay disciplined in the face of this 'adolescent consciousness'—commonly described as childish behaviour. This self-discipline is needed to avoid reacting spontaneously to 'attacks' or allowing our ego to be triggered. Otherwise, we immediately fall into the trap of behaving in exactly the same way as the toxic person. We will emerge from any such encounter feeling angry, guilty and miserable because we are not sure to what extent we were responsible for damaging whatever relationship there may have been.

Equally helpful in cases where we cannot keep away from the toxic person and whose company we might otherwise enjoy (for example, a relative or friend) is *Key Strategy 2, knowing who we are* and being comfortable in one's own skin. We will be less anxious, more compassionate and less likely to be triggered. Being emotionally self-aware enables us to act from relaxed consciousness and not anxious compulsion. We thus deal better with such situations when they occur—in a calm, respectful yet considered and firm manner.

However, if we wish to establish a modus vivendi that is acceptable to us, *Key Strategy 5, being assertive*, will be the best ultimate course of action. We should explain how we feel when confronted with this behaviour. We need to be open and sincere, without judgment or anger, and ask for collaboration in its resolution (*Key Strategy 6, focus on solutions*). This gives us the best chances of success.

Since this toxic behaviour pattern has been learned and is habitual, it will be necessary to be patient. Be prepared to repeat this response. Each time, explain how it affects our feelings and why it upsets the relationship and the friendship.

In a *business context* (for example, as the supervisor of such a person), this toxicity must be addressed as soon as possible. Our assertive conversation (*Key Strategy 5*) must include a clear explanation of their behaviour and an equally clear request for change. If possible, offer help in the form of coaching or therapy.

Nothing will work, however, unless the toxic person *recognizes* that they are indeed behaving in a negative and counter-productive way and *accepts* responsibility for change.

This clear, calm but uncompromising conversation must not be avoided. It is the duty of the leader to exercise their responsibility and initiate the process, for the good of the wider group. It may not work. The toxic person may be unwilling to address their career-limiting issue. In this case, more robust action becomes inevitable and necessary. But an honest attempt to make things work must be seriously and conscientiously attempted first.

In both the personal and business contexts, it should be remembered that people exhibiting these traits *lack self-confidence.* They find it difficult to trust others because they cannot trust themselves. Their lack of self-belief is matched by a view of the world as a generally inimical and unfriendly place. The cup is half empty rather than half full and they look out for signals that support their view.

As a result, they will tend to be underachievers and will be loath to complete tasks for fear of failure and blame. Not surprisingly, therefore, they do not have much fun, do not laugh very often and find it almost impossible to laugh at themselves.

> Love who you are and what you are and what you do.
> Laugh at yourself and at life and nothing can touch you.
>
> —Louise Hay

> Man suffers only because he takes seriously what the Gods made for fun.
>
> —Alan Watts

PART 4

Case Studies

23

Introduction to Case Studies

The following case studies are designed to demonstrate how the seven Key Strategies for dealing with toxic people or toxic situations are applied in real life. Every case is based on genuine situations and events but, for reasons of confidentiality, names, genders and other details have been changed and some editorial licence has been taken in order to render the teachings more generally applicable.

Readers should be able to easily relate to some, if not all of the studies, and to appreciate the context in which the toxicity occurs. It will then be possible to draw the lessons and take the advice that is suggested. It will be found that almost all the seven pieces of advice apply to some extent in each case. The most important advice relating to each case is, however, made clear.

24

Toxic Committee Team Member

Case Study A

Key Strategies: Be assertive (5),
look for solutions (6), build great relationships (7)

Background

Lewis had been an active member of the charity for many years and had contributed greatly to its success. He had spent long hours in dedicated service, promoting and defending the charity with local councils and government bodies. He had animated fund-raising activities, hosted and managed events and produced information leaflets supporting the charity. Well-known and well respected within the charity and the community, Lewis was dynamic and well-intentioned and had amassed a considerable body of knowledge of the ins and outs of the charity and its systems. He had even developed his own concepts and activities.

The problem was that Lewis increasingly felt that he was the only competent person on the charity committee. He believed his colleagues were all rather weak, unprofessional and generally incapable of taking sensible decisions without his input and help. This extended to criticising the minutes of meetings he had not attended and subsequently reversing decisions that had been made by the committee in his absence. If necessary, he would simply plough ahead with his ideas and initiate activities and payments for matters that had not been agreed. Moreover, he felt increasingly unloved and unacknowledged—despite all his efforts and long hours.

The result of this toxicity was that he often became disrespectful to fellow committee members and the chair. Argumentative and didactic during meetings, he was increasingly rude and arrogant both face to face and in correspondence. He frequently rewrote recommendations or proposals. In his considered opinion, the work and decisions of the committee were amateurish, while his work was neither properly recognized nor praised.

Meetings of the committee, which were otherwise polite, friendly and positive, frequently became unpleasantly conflictual and tense affairs when he attended. A toxic atmosphere pervaded the room from the start. New committee members recruited to the team were put off serving. Some rapidly withdrew, declined to attend or resigned, indicating clearly that this was not the sort of environment that they wished to work in.

People who might be very helpful to the committee refused to join, while others reluctantly struggled on but did not enjoy the experience. Meetings of the committee were anticipated with trepidation. The only time there seemed to be harmony and a friendly, constructive atmosphere, with the rapid resolution of most items on the agenda, was when Lewis was absent.

Causes of this toxicity

Regrettably, cases of this type (based on a true situation) are commonplace in both voluntary and corporate organizations.

Many people do indeed contribute many hours of their time, over many years, to voluntary organizations. Their knowledge, commitment and energy is invaluable—not least because often a small number of people do most of the work. But if someone begins to feel that they are indispensable and behaves in a bullying, didactic and arrogant way, problems quickly emerge. Any potential good is offset (often eliminated) by the negativity caused by ego-derived, toxic behaviour.

Counter-intuitively, given its aggression and drive, this behaviour illustrates a chronic lack of self-confidence and self-worth. Such people have a huge need to be in control as well as needing regular 'stroking'. Their egos are telling them that unless they behave aggressively and get their way, they are no longer of value. They have created an image of themselves as the knowledgeable saviours of the institution and its potential destruction is terrifying. Always better, in their eyes, to be unpopular and 'right' than to go along with everyone else and be 'invisible'.

Being difficult is a way of gaining, regaining or holding attention. The starving ego needs feeding and craves acknowledgment. It needs to be in charge, to be right, to be admired and respected. Perversely, it also craves love.

However, meeting the demands of ego is to invite and create conflict. The cost and impact of such egotistic behaviour is disharmony, dysfunctionality and disappointment for *everyone else*. What may have begun with the best of intentions (contributing to a successful project) has been entirely hijacked by ego and becomes highly destructive.

In the words of the English proverb:

The road to hell is paved with good intentions.

How to address the situation using Key Strategies

The first question to ask is: *Where is the prime responsibility for finding a resolution?*

Because this is a committee, the chairperson (equivalent of first line supervisor in a business context) is responsible for addressing the issue. If we look at the Key Strategies, number 1, keeping away, is unlikely to be an option. However, *Key Strategy 2, know who you are*, will be of immeasurable help and importance to the chairperson. This will enable them *to stay calm, to not react* or allow themselves to be triggered (*Key Strategy 3*) so they can respond by appropriately *establishing boundaries* (*Key Strategy 4*) *assertively* (*5*).

Key Strategies 2, 3, 4 and 5 are about knowing how to handle conflict without allowing ego to be triggered. They allow the chairperson to then *focus on solutions* (*6*) in a highly toxic situation such as this. It will also be crucial to *build great relationships* (*7*) by listening to the advice of other team members and soliciting their all-important support when key decisions are taken.

The chairperson needs to clarify their objective and strategy. Their prime objective must be to maintain or restore the harmony of the team so that the business of the committee can be conducted smoothly and effectively. Secondly, they should aim to find a solution that allows Lewis to continue as a member and make valuable contributions to the committee based on his undoubted knowledge and experience, but *without* his toxic, disruptive behaviour.

If this cannot be achieved, however, the chairperson has to be prepared to decide how best to remove Lewis from the committee.

Having carefully considered as much verbal and written evidence as possible (the input and advice from other committee members (*Key Strategy 7*)), the chairperson should initiate a private off-line conversation with Lewis as soon as possible.

They should be *assertive* and sincere (*Key Strategy 5*) throughout and address the issue openly, constructively, without embarrassment or drama (which would signal a triggering of ego). They should make clear that, while Lewis's knowledge and experience are highly valued and appreciated, his behaviour is causing disquiet and disharmony. It is harming the committee's effectiveness, for which, as chairperson, they are responsible and accountable.

The chairperson should emphasize that it is their role to ensure that the committee functions properly and, thus, that all committee members are equally and fully respected and their views heard. When decisions are taken (unanimously or by majority vote) they should be accepted in good grace by all. This is the spirit of collective responsibility. If any member is unable to attend a meeting, they can make their views known in advance to any other member who will represent them. They will then be bound by any decision taken in their absence. Not all decisions will necessarily have the approval of all members. That is perfectly normal and accepted as part of a committee structure. If everyone thought the same way over every issue, all but one of the committee would be redundant!

The chairperson should listen politely to Lewis's comments and responses. (These are likely to include everything from disbelief to outright rejection of any responsibility for the issue and include the belief that all the other members lack sufficient knowledge or professionalism to make meaningful contributions.) However, the chairperson *should not accept or condone* (under any circumstances) any excuse for bad or disrespectful behaviour. Nor should they indulge in gossip or blame games or stray from the matter in hand. They should keep strictly and calmly to the facts of the issue itself and the respective responsibilities of the chairperson and committee members.

This means that the '*what*' of the problem needs to be raised and acknowledged *first*. This must not be avoided or allowed to be set aside or diverted in any way. Until the 'what' has been thoroughly *exposed and accepted* as being the issue, the chairperson should not move on to the next stage. It will not be possible to explore solutions if the problem has not first been accepted!

When the 'what' has been aired and accepted, the chairperson can move on to examining the 'how' of improving and resolving the situation.

What to do if the toxic person does not accept they are the problem

It may be that (despite proper discussion) Lewis cannot accept that his behaviour is problematic and continues to believe problems all lie elsewhere. He says it is other people who do not understand him and he refuses to address or modify his behaviour. In this case, the chairperson will need to be prepared to remove him from the committee. In preparation for this, they will need to know what the procedure is for removing members and consult the charity's statutes. If there is no written procedure, the chair will ultimately need to ask Lewis to resign.

How to look for solutions

Hopefully, Lewis will accept that he has an issue that needs to be resolved. In this case, the chairperson can move the conversation forward to the 'how' of resolution, the *focus on solutions* (*Key Strategy 6*). The aim is to re-establish harmony and wellbeing in the committee, as well as accommodate Lewis's needs, where they are justified and possible.

The objective of this next stage is to create a 'contract' between the chairperson and Lewis regarding Lewis's behaviour at future meetings. This would include: speaking in turn; not interrupting when others speak; accepting majority decisions; presenting his own verbal and written views diplomatically and politely; supporting other team members; and accepting that everyone is entitled to have their view and their say. The chairperson could also agree to meet with Lewis ahead of meetings if there are items relevant to his expertise.

Once a 'contract' is established, which will include *the setting of clear boundaries* (*Key Strategy 4*), the chairperson should be especially vigilant about ensuring that it is adhered to. At subsequent meetings, the chairperson should remain diplomatic and *stay calm* (*Key Strategy 3*). He should be polite but also clear and robust on insisting that Lewis adhere to their mutually agreed moral contract.

It is initially helpful for the chairperson to set up a separate, private meeting with Lewis in advance of the formal meeting, in order to go over potentially contentious issues. They can also establish a follow-up session after the committee meeting to review progress. Assuming all goes well, this need only happen once or twice.

In similar cases, where the toxic individual has *fully accepted* to receive guidance and coaching, we have also found it useful to establish an agreed private signal between the chair and the member. If the chair feels that the member is starting to transgress the boundary, they make this known. The signal can be very simple—for example, tapping a pen discreetly on the table while looking at the member—but should be a recognisable reminder of the 'contract'.

The role of other team members

It is not acceptable for committee members to opt out of taking responsibility for helping to resolve the issue. All team members have a responsibility to help the process of re-establishing good working relationships within the group (*Key Strategy 7, build great relationships*). They should support the chairperson and offer advice, if appropriate. This is best done in private. In this example, they should speak with the chairperson and make clear their disapproval of Lewis's behaviour and the need to address the issue. If they have experienced a similar issue, they should provide advice on dealing with it.

At meetings, they should follow *Key Strategies 2* and *3—know who you are*, and *stay calm*—and remain composed and self-aware, not allowing themselves to be triggered. They should approach agenda items factually rather than emotionally and should focus on outcomes and solutions (*Key Strategy 6, focus on solutions*). They should not reply directly to aggressive comments (verbal or written), but, if appropriate, counter them by concentrating just on the facts as they see them.

If circumstances do not improve, they will be best advised to apply *Key Strategy 1, to keep their distance.* They can either resign or decline to be re-elected. Life is too short for wasting energy on toxic situations such as these.

> Life is too short, and the time we waste in yawning never can be regained.
>
> —Stendhal

Understanding the toxic individual

In this case, Lewis is clearly a knowledgeable and experienced person who has made considerable and beneficial contributions to the work of the charity in the past. He also clearly has the capacity to continue to do so in the future. He is well-intentioned. Beneath that dogmatic and difficult exterior (stoked by an overactive ego) lurks a kind and gentle soul longing to be appreciated and loved.

When he feels good about himself—when he feels acknowledged and in control—he can be highly productive. The problem is that to feel 'in charge', Lewis resorts to toxic behaviour that unsettles everyone else in a manner that is intolerable. The challenge, therefore, is to maintain the positive aspects of Lewis's personality while dampening down or eliminating the toxic behaviour that often accompanies it.

Lewis appears to have a personality disorder that would benefit from professional counselling. He needs to discover, face and resolve what are probably deep-seated issues. Erratic, angry, selfish, autocratic behaviour has many possible causes, which can be attributed to unresolved underlying psychological issues and trauma. This trauma is causing him considerable personal stress and unhappiness. It will almost certainly already have affected his mental and physical health and wellbeing—not to mention that of his immediate family and friends.

This may also be associated with the side-effect of medicines and/or a stressful, unhealthy lifestyle, as well as personal or family problems. This is the domain of professional cognitive, psycho- and hypno-therapists.

A friend or respected committee member should find the right opportunity to raise this possibility with Lewis in a kind, helpful and compassionate way and encourage him to seek professional help. The alternative for Lewis is to continue a life of suffering and pain, which will have disastrous mental and physical effects.

> Mental health problems don't define who you are. They are something you experience. You walk in the rain, and you feel the rain, but, importantly, you are not the rain.
>
> —Matt Haig

25

The Toxic Boss

Case Study B

Key Strategies: Set boundaries (4), be assertive (5)

Background

Steven worked as a senior project manager for a leading city-based consulting company in a major financial centre. He was diligent, meticulous, hard-working, highly talented and successful. He was capable of managing (highly lucrative) complex projects to the considerable satisfaction of the customer. Customers appreciated him and asked for him to work on their business. He was well liked and respected by all who came into contact with him.

Steven worked long hours and stayed late, compensating for the chronic shortage of support staff. This shortage was a problem he had repeatedly raised with his boss, Joan, who promised to fix the problem but never did.

The company was constituted as a partnership, in which the partners shared the residual profits. This meant the partners were very conscious of costs, which represented their income and wealth. Increasing staff numbers reduced profits. A fine line needed to be struck between employing sufficient staff to deliver customer satisfaction and profits. Shortfalls in manpower were regularly made up by existing staff working longer hours—frequently at the expense of their physical and mental health. This issue is endemic to the industry.

An additional problem was that Steven's boss, Joan, did not seem to approve of Steven or of his work. Nor did she try to alleviate his crowded work schedule. She would change deadlines at short notice, requiring Steven to work late even just before weekends. She openly criticized his work and refused to procure additional staff even for lucrative projects. In addition, she gave Steven mediocre reviews—even though it was widely recognized that Steven was a highly talented 'must keep' executive. Her general lack of respect caused Steven to become increasingly anxious and unhappy. The unhappiness was carried over to the home where it was shared with his (fortunately very understanding) partner, who empathised with the symptoms of stress and helped to soften Steven's pain.

Seeking Potential Solutions to a Toxic Situation

Steven and his partner realized that the stress of the bullying was damaging Steven's health and wellbeing. He was suffering sleepless nights, tiredness and other symptoms of anxiety. His natural enthusiasm was being dampened and he began dreading going to work. Together they looked at possible solutions, such as consulting HR, having a direct conversation with Joan and consulting with Joan's boss.

He began with the human resources department. They said they could not help as this was a matter that could only be resolved between Steven and the partner (Joan). They were effectively powerless to intervene.

Next, Steven repeatedly tried to approach an elusive and impatient Joan to explain why the lack of adequate resources was affecting completion times and what needed to be done. She would indicate agreement to the need, but no concrete action happened. And her behaviour continued unchanged.

Steven also questioned the reasons for the mediocre performance review. Joan claimed they were due to delayed completion times. Yet these were in large part due to the lack of resources—despite Steven's attempts to compensate by working extensive additional hours during the week and at weekends. There seemed little likelihood of breaking the vicious cycle.

How the Toxic Situation Resolved

Steven, however, was very highly valued by the client, who realized the critical role that he played. When Joan raised reassigning responsibilities, the client insisted categorically that Steven continue to work on their project. The client was well aware of Steven's frustration.

Fearful that Steven might be moved off their business, the client decided to open a dialogue with Steven with a view to having him join their company. They realized that they could not afford to lose the linchpin of the project! Moreover, he estimated that the switch of employer would not be disadvantageous to Steven's current company since the day-to-day work would remain with them. Steven, as project leader, would now become a client rather than a supplier!

Steven declined the idea several times—partly from a sense of loyalty and partly out of fear of the unknown. However, the client made increasingly attractive offers—in terms of roles and responsibilities and financially. After careful consideration, Steven, who had realized that Joan's negative, bullying behaviour would not change, accepted the offer. After experiencing some moments of trepidation, Steven felt considerable relief. And the transfer was effected smoothly and without negative repercussions.

The great loss, of course, was to Steven's original company. The big challenge for business today is the acquisition and retention of talent. It is in short supply and critical to success. This makes it very costly to lose talent, not only due to the value they bring to their work, but also because recruiting and training replacements is expensive.

When a company has talented individuals such as Steven in their team, it is foolhardy to lose them—especially as a result of basic managerial failings. Steven's original company clearly has no effective process for managing and retaining talent. Its HR policies are ineffectual and largely bureaucratic and there is inadequate or non-existent leadership and motivational skills training. The company undervalues the human dimension, focusing almost exclusively on short-term profitability.

How the Key Strategies could have been used

Steven ultimately chose *Key Strategy 1, avoid toxicity and keep your distance*, but only after being subjected to a very long period of abusive treatment by his toxic boss, Joan. In putting up with this for such a long time, Steven demonstrates that he does not *know who he is* (*Key Strategy 2*), while his constant state of anxiety reveals that he is not comfortable in his skin. He has most probably never spent any quiet time thinking about this!

While he *has* been able to apply *Key Strategy 3, stay calm*, his discussions with Joan revealed inadequate *assertiveness* (*Key Strategy 5*) and the absence of any attempt to *establish boundaries* (*Key Strategy 4*).

Although attempts were made to *find solutions* (*Key Strategy 6*), the absence of assertiveness or boundary setting with Joan meant that the search for solutions was predominantly with third parties, notably HR. *Key Strategy 7, build great relationships,* was well applied with regard to home life and an understanding partner but clearly deficient as regards managing 'upwards'.

In conclusion, Steven has a wonderful opportunity in his new company and role to start afresh. However, he risks a repetition of the same situation until he has learned the skills of managing toxic people properly—especially *Key Strategies 2, 4, 5* and *7.*

The lessons the toxic boss and the company should learn

Some of the lessons have already been alluded to above but are worth reiterating. Joan is in need of leadership training. This must include a full EQ analysis and training on: self-awareness; how to create a safe, empathetic and motivating environment; active listening skills; and all the lessons pertaining to managing toxic people and situations as described in *Toxicum.*

Joan has done the company a great disservice with her role in losing a high potential employee. Whoever appointed Joan is also in need of similar training. Since this lack of leadership awareness appears to be prevalent throughout the organisation, the entire company should review their people development programs—especially their leadership development. The company should also reconsider the importance of the human dimension. Without this nothing of value can be sustainably created. It is a crucial part of their overall customer-centric purpose.

26

The Toxic Sibling

Case Study C

Key Strategies: Set boundaries (4), be assertive (5)

Background

Jayne's brother, Sam, suffers from anxiety disorder. He has persistent worries and fears about everyday situations, feels nervous and tense and has a constant sense of dread and impending doom. He sleeps poorly and has regular night sweats. He cannot think of anything other than his present worries and has trouble concentrating. He also has occasional panic attacks. This condition has inevitably affected his career.

To create some sense of order in his life, he has become something of a control freak. Everything needs to be structured and organized and he has developed rules and routines for everything. He insists on these routines—however inappropriate and unnecessary they appear to other people. 'A place for everything and everything in its place' is his mantra.

Sam's family have fully accepted that he suffers from anxiety and leave him free to do whatever he wants in his own home (where he lives alone). Unfortunately, he displays the same behaviour when he visits Jayne and other members of the family.

At her home, he will spontaneously move furniture, adjust trinkets, change place settings and adjust ornaments if he thinks they are 'not straight'. He has been known to rearrange books in the bookshelf so that they are at more coherent heights. He also puts on music irrespective of whether anyone wants it or not.

Sam's need to exercise control extends to family events, which he insists on organizing—even though this gives him severe anxiety and creates conflict within the family. He will not listen to the needs or opinions of others and belittles disagreements as a lack of family loyalty.

Sam is a highly toxic worrier who has allowed his anxiety to determine his identity and the course of his life. He is 'out of control' and his behaviour is disturbing and disruptive. He is difficult to live with, angers and triggers others easily and creates an atmosphere of fear and tension whenever he is around.

How to manage a toxic family member using Key Strategies

Although Sam is toxic, he is still a family member. While *Key Strategy 1, recognize toxicity and avoid,* would be the usual first recommendation, this may not be possible with a family member. (Although it may be possible to limit the frequency of visits and events.) So Key Strategies 2 and 3, know who you are and stay calm, become that much more important.

Key Strategy 2, know who you are, also implies a level of maturity, self-awareness and empathy. These are essential in situations such as this where there is a need for sympathy and understanding, as well as patience. The fact is that Sam is a family member who is suffering from a mental health illness. While his behaviour can be infuriating and distressing, he is nevertheless a human being and a relative in need of help and support.

Family members need to follow *Key Strategy 3, stay calm,* and avoid being triggered by Sam's behaviour. However understandable, becoming angered and frustrated will worsen the situation for everybody. A high level of self-control and maturity as well as a sense of compassion for Sam are essential.

It is very important for Jayne to speak with Sam, while following *Key Strategy 5, be assertive*. She must address Sam's illness openly, sympathetically and in a straightforward, unembarrassed manner, using 'I' and 'we' statements. The objective is to recommend that Sam seek professional treatment for his condition, which is affecting his health and his family and their health. He will *not* be able to deal with it himself.

The fundamental reasons that have led to his condition have been with him and festering for many years. He will need help to understand and then deal with them. Psychotherapy and hypnotherapy would undoubtedly help. The family love him as their brother, son, grandson or uncle, but find his behaviour distressing and dysfunctional. He needs to understand this and fully accept that he should address the matter. Until he does, nothing will change. On the contrary, things are likely to get worse.

What to do if the toxic relative does not accept the need to get professional help

If Sam neither accepts that he has a problem nor that he needs to seek treatment, then the family will need to apply *Key Strategy 4, set clear boundaries*. For example, when Sam visits Jayne's home, one of the boundaries might be that they agree together in advance what music to play, and that Sam desists from rearranging her furniture. However, it might also be agreed that he may readjust the books in her bookshelf, but that is the limit of his boundary.

The family might also wish to set boundaries for the organisation of family events. This could be that they will agree together (or in a smaller subgroup) what the event should entail and who does what. Sam will be one voice among several. They could also agree that no event will happen outside this process.

There are many ways to set boundaries (even ceasing contact for a period of time). It is up to those concerned to establish them carefully and in accordance with the need. This means that *Key Strategy 6, focus on solutions*, is essential, as is involving Sam—not least to obtain his 'buy-in'.

Equally essential will be to adhere to the boundaries set!

If a boundary is established and then abandoned, not only does this invalidate the process, but it makes things worse. It will reinforce Sam's belief that he is surrounded by people who have no mind of their own and need to be controlled! Such a course of action will be of no help to Sam.

27

The Toxic Partner

Case Study D

Key Strategies: Recognize toxicity and avoid (1), know who you are (2), set boundaries (4), build great relationships (7)

Background

Andy and Caroline met at their gym. Although Andy was married, he was in the process of divorcing and suggested to Caroline that they meet up for coffee. This led to further dates and a deeper relationship began. Andy had a demanding, high-profile and stressful job. This was coupled with an acrimonious impending divorce, involving the custody of a daughter. Caroline was still recovering from a recent divorce herself. She was finding her feet—still sensitive, vulnerable and suffering from low self-esteem.

Over the course of the next few weeks, Andy began to 'love bomb' Caroline. He sent her flowers on a weekly basis, texted her excessively flattering messages and showered her with attention and affection. Although Caroline was initially somewhat reticent and cautious, she gradually bought into the relationship. She was overjoyed with the attention and apparent kindness, after her recent traumatic experience. They began a serious relationship and became seemingly inseparable.

During these first months, Andy revealed many of his fears and insecurities to Caroline. She reciprocated, sharing with him all the pain and hurt of her previous relationship. A close bond developed between them, and she felt she had known him all her life. They would talk for hours. He told her he loved her and hoped they could begin a new life together, maybe have a child, all as soon as his divorce was finalised.

During one of Andy's most stressful work occasions, when he was seriously anxious about his ability to deliver, Caroline looked after him with great tenderness and care. She successfully helped him through the trauma. She gradually devoted more and more time to him and his needs. She invested heavily in the relationship and had high expectations for the future. She was in love with him.

It is difficult to say when things started to go wrong. After a while, Caroline began to feel that the more she gave Andy, the more he seemed to want. For example, she would stay at his place, but he began to expect her to look after it while he was away—feeding and cleaning the dog and doing chores for him. Caroline happily agreed because she was convinced that they were in love and had a romantic and blissful future to look forward to.

At the same time, it did gradually dawn on Caroline that they had some very different interests and values. However, she was undeterred. If anyone suggested to her that she might be falling into a potential and painful trap, they would be roundly criticised as overcautious, cynical and jealous of her happiness. Or else she would refuse to discuss the matter, saying that she did not want any more conflict. She would say that she knew what the problem was and that she would be able to deal with it.

To her old friends and family, Caroline became more and more isolated, elusive and withdrawn. She cancelled engagements and meetings at the last minute—often at Andy's request. She became disorientated regarding her own activities, which he considered trivial and meaningless. His divorce was proceeding very slowly. His wife and daughter made it very clear that they resented Caroline and felt she was a bad influence on Andy. They blamed her for anything that went wrong with Andy and his daughter refused to see him with her.

Moreover, Andy's treatment of Caroline became increasingly overbearing, disrespectful, even brutal. He would get drunk and swear at her. He would go out with friends without telling her or asking her to accompany him. He would fly into a rage if they met by chance in town, saying that she had no right to be there or intrude on him and his friends. To add insult to injury, he dated another woman. And then bought a new house on his own—not even consulting her in the process.

The morning after insulting Caroline and treating her very unkindly, he would apologise profusely, promise never to do it again and repeat his desire to be married and have a family with her. But this atonement would always be very short lived. Before too long, Andy's toxic behaviour would restart.

Caroline's disappointment and unhappiness increased with every blow. She had invested so much in a person she had come to love and with whom she saw such a bright future. She became depressed and lost weight. Her interest in life declined and she was frequently in tears. Andy remained impervious to her suffering—frequently adding to it though his selfish and devastatingly cruel words and actions.

In spite of all her pain, Caroline persevered in trying to make the relationship work. Even though, in her heart of hearts, she knew that it was doomed, she believed that she would be able, eventually, to change Andy and bring him round.

During the next few months, she would leave, only to return as soon as he said a few nice things. She then worked even harder to regain the 'honeymoon' phase of their relationship. Her life became a series of brief highs followed by increasingly painful lows.

The turning point came when Andy's business transferred him abroad. The assignment was for an indeterminate period, at least several months. Whenever he returned for a weekend, he exhibited the same toxic behaviour as before. He then asked her to come and stay with him. After a couple of short, joyless trips, Caroline recognised that moving abroad permanently would mean abandoning her son. She declined to follow Andy.

The space provided by his absence allowed her to find some clarity about who Andy really was. She saw the true nature of his narcissistic behaviour and motives. With sadness but courageously, she reluctantly accepted that the relationship was over and decided to leave Andy permanently. She realized that, in his head, he had already left *her* many months before.

Understanding the main features of this toxic relationship

This case study is in no way unique. It is replayed across the world with a great many couples. The causes and effects are very similar. A study conducted in the US in 2017 found that narcissistic abuse had affected over 158 million people in their lifetime.

In our case, Andy is a narcissist and narcissism is an extreme form of toxicity. He suffers from narcissistic personality disorder, with antisocial personality disorder features. This means he has an overblown sense of entitlement and the need to exploit others, while also being admired. He lacks empathy and maturity, feels superior to others and is callously and remorselessly abusive. Like all bullies with exaggerated egos, he has poor self-esteem and is frightened of 'failure', which he compensates for with his manipulative cruelty. Being physically attractive, he exudes charm when it is in his interest to do so. However, he lacks socially relevant emotions or any sense of morality.

Narcissists are highly manipulative and abusive and are the cause of much domestic violence. On the surface, they can appear to be very fine. They can easily be seen as outstanding members of their communities and companies, while causing great pain and suffering both at home and in the workplace. They can turn on the charm, with a magnetic charisma that can fool anyone. They are very difficult to treat psychologically (not least since they rarely accept that they are at fault or in need of remediation) and are highly dangerous.

How to manage a toxic narcissist using Key Strategies

It is very easy to fall prey to psychopathic narcissists. This is especially true for empathetic, kind and helpful people since their greatest assets are easily used against them by unscrupulous and malignantly toxic people. This is even more the case if the victim is vulnerable.

Toxic narcissists like Andy will use all kinds of manipulative tactics to lure and control their victim. These tactics include: *stonewalling* (to silence and create deep discomfort and incredulity);

gaslighting (to erode the sense of reality and encourage feelings of blame and guilt); *love bombing* (to disarm through overwhelming flattery and attention), *intermittent reinforcement* (to keep the victim believing that it will all be alright in the end, encouraging them to obsessively redouble their efforts); *shaming* (to destabilize and reinforce guilt); *poor me protesting* (to elicit sympathy); *projecting* (their negative feelings on to their victim); *premature intimacy* (to promote bonding); and *post-relationship control*, or *hoovering* (to suck the victim back after the end of the relationship').

In this case study, many of the above tactics were applied, but especially love bombing, premature intimacy, intermittent reinforcement and hoovering. How could they be countered using the Key Strategies?

Since Caroline was fully aware that she was still in a vulnerable state following the breakdown of her own relationship, she should clearly have applied *Key Strategy 1, recognize toxicity and avoid*. The ideal time would have been as soon as she had learnt of Andy's current marital situation and problems and when he started to love bomb her. If not at that point, she should have definitely been extra vigilant when he acted the 'poor me', looking for sympathy and gentleness.

However, in the words of the philosopher Blaise Pascal:

> *Le coeur a ses raisons, que la raison ne connaît point.*
>
> (The heart has its reasons, that reason [rationality] cannot explain.)

Caroline's application of *Key Strategy 2, master yourself, know who you are*, and her high level of maturity and self-awareness did undoubtedly help her keep her sanity. These qualities allowed her to understand clearly and with considerable patience, empathy and compassion, what was happening. However, knowing who you are is more than just an intellectual exercise. It requires a depth of emotional perception and the ability to rise above the emotional entanglement of romantic attachments—however difficult that is.

To regain our power to determine the course of our life and its happiness, we need to deeply realize that: we are all interconnected, interdependent; we are not separate individuals; and true love is absolute and not 'dual' (meaning love and its dual opposite, hate, have become pure love without an opposite). We have to learn to detach ourselves from desires and cravings that are the cause of so much suffering. We must also accept that self-respect, self-esteem and self-love are more important than any unworthy human attachments.

When we are no longer dependent on others or allow others to control our emotions, we are free. This freedom enables us to withdraw more easily from toxic relationships, which do us no good, and find relationships that are more honest, authentic, reciprocal, understanding and, above all, loving.

Key Strategy 3, stay calm, do not react, was something Caroline did as well as could be expected. She preferred to withdraw rather than fight, although this would leave her feeling dejected, deflated and very unhappy. Staying calm with toxic people is very important, but especially when it is combined with *Key Strategies 4* and *5, set clear boundaries* and *be assertive*, which are the most important competences to bring to bear in these highly difficult circumstances. It is critically important to set clear boundaries with toxic people *and with oneself.* Do not to accept any deviation from them!

When excessive attention and love bombing occurs at the beginning of any relationship, it is fine to accept and be flattered by the compliments. However, do not invest too much too soon in someone who is barely known. Relationships and trust take time to build, with evidence of respect and trustworthiness.

Be on the look-out for clear warning signals of a toxic relationship: attempts to coerce; desire to control; speeding up the relationship in a way that feels uncomfortable; signs of irritation or anger; excessive drinking; selfishness; and meanness of any kind.

All relationships have their ups and downs. That is entirely normal, and in many ways desirable. Each partner has to explore and learn to truly understand the other—once the initial masked initiation dance comes to an end. But it is the way in which differences are addressed and how love is expressed by both partners in this process that is the determinant factor.

With toxic narcissists it is often very difficult to apply *Key Strategy 6, focus on solutions*, since such people tend to be 'my way or no way'. This win/lose ultimatum is impossible to resolve.

However, *Key Strategy 7, build great relationships*, is particularly important in circumstances such as this one. Reliable friends and family who can maintain objectivity and who truly have the interests of the victim at heart are indispensable. They are sources of help, support, encouragement, advice and sanity.

Being gaslighted has the effect of making victims doubt themselves. This can be readily exposed and eliminated by the reality checks of trusted friends and family. While the pain of being abused by a toxic narcissist is very real, true friends will rally around to provide essential comfort and love and help with the healing process.

28

The Toxic Leader

Case Study E

Key Strategies: Keep calm (3), set boundaries (4), look for solutions (6), build great relationships (7)

Background

Martin had always been diligent and conscientious throughout his career and had worked himself up the corporate ladder to become the head of a major division.

His results were good—although it was acknowledged that he had benefitted from the work of some very competent predecessors. He had not sought to make any dramatic change but rather to continue with the previous strategy.

His superiors found him somewhat obsequious when he reported to them and his choice of unusual and rather fussy words when addressing anyone would frequently raise an eyebrow and a smile. But his business results were fine, and his somewhat self-centred personality was not creating any obviously negative issues. His traits were viewed as quirky rather than problematic. He was always impeccably turned out and took great care of his appearance.

Titles and status were important to him as well as the trappings of seniority on which he would insist. He was highly respectful and convivial with his superiors.

As the division for which he was responsible started to face greater commercial headwinds, Martin's behaviour, which had always been correct and pleasant when things were going well, began to change. He became increasingly stressed and anxious. His previously calm exterior would dissolve and be replaced by frustration and panic, which soon turned to occasional fits of anger. Martin became increasingly aggressive and dictatorial in his dealings with colleagues. He would issue instructions before a full discussion had taken place and countermand decisions made by his executive team colleagues.

When colleagues suggested meeting to discuss the best strategy to follow, he refused to listen. Instead, he told his colleagues that they needed to deliver on the original budget commitment—even though it was increasingly obvious that circumstances had evolved such that the original budget could not be achieved. (The original budget had itself been established 'top down' without the participation of the team.) Nevertheless, Martin started to blame them for the poor performance. He insisted that they work harder and smarter and that their employees work later and over weekends to make up any shortfalls. His fear at not delivering and at being seen to have failed was projected on to his team, who he held responsible for these problems.

Although he had previously been punctilious in arriving on time to meetings, and expecting others to do the same, Martin began either missing meetings or arriving late, without apology or explanation. As far as he was concerned, appearing or not appearing at meetings was 'his' decision. He was entitled to do what he wanted. He began to stay in his office for longer periods of time. He rejected outright the suggestion that it was important to be visible in times of difficulty. He had no wish to listen and explain, to encourage and support and to show alignment and solidarity with his immediate team and their employees. Everyone should just 'keep quiet and get on with it'.

When his superiors began asking questions about the performance and what plans were afoot to address them, Martin indicated that he had lost confidence in several members of his team. He felt changes needed to be made. They had underdelivered on their obligations and were not up to the task.

His proposal was to fire two of them with immediate effect and find two replacements (either from another division or from outside). When he began the process of 'letting one of them go', he said that the decision was head office's and not his. The team became increasingly demoralised and agreed to meet together to decide what they should do. The question they were asking themselves was: How best to deal with such a toxic 'leader'?

Poor leadership and its consequences

Before we consider what Key Strategies the team should apply, it is worth reflecting on leadership in business and other walks of life. The regrettable fact is that leadership is not regularly taught in schools, universities or, systematically, in business. The more enlightened schools, who have managed to create some space in the curriculum, do give students some instruction on leadership. And activities such as Outward Bound courses and Duke of Edinburgh awards also provide elements of leadership. However, by university level the focus is generally on specific faculty subjects. Despite some opportunities, the reality is that it is expected that leaders will 'emerge'—as if by some natural process.

When students join a business or other institution, courses are provided, but there is little consistent leadership skills or excellence instruction and no real follow-up. Business schools have many courses available, but companies use these relatively sparingly because of their cost. Even then they are of short duration with little opportunity for practice.

As a result, there are very few role models. Look across the wider leadership of major political, academic and service institutions. The dearth of real role models is glaring. The same lack is found among celebrities, on TV programmes and social media. Not surprisingly, perhaps the best place to find leadership instruction is in the military, which provides officers with training over at least three years. (We have seen remarkable evidence of this first-hand from visiting the Royal Navy at the Portsmouth base, as well as during regular conversations with serving and former military officers.)

Leadership is a critical quality whatever the circumstance and is vital whenever a group of people are assembled to complete a task. Leadership requires high levels of EQ, maturity, listening and caring, as well as a bias towards action and timeliness. It also requires discipline, courage and self-motivation, as well as enthusiasm. It has to demonstrate a positive attitude with the ability to inspire, especially in times of hardship. Setting the right example is fundamental to this and to inspiring following generations.

Leadership, above all, entails a very high level of responsibility—for colleagues, employees, customers, suppliers, investors, local communities, the environment and the families of stakeholders. Decisions taken may have very far-reaching implications and can never be taken without proper consideration of all these factors. Leadership is about service to others, not service to oneself. When a position of leadership is attained, it is not the achievement of an end goal, but the beginning of a new chapter of service.

How to manage a toxic leader using Key Strategies

Martin's team (his employees) have been placed in a very difficult position. Their business is deteriorating and their boss appears to be drowning. In his panicked desire to protect himself, he is placing their jobs at risk.

Key Strategy 1, keep your distance, is clearly not possible. And although Key Strategy 2, know who you are, is always of value in maintaining internal mental stability, the urgency of the situation makes it impracticable here.

Key Strategy 7, build great relationships, and *Key Strategy 6, focus on solutions*, are the most immediately useful strategies. The team's first imperative is to ensure that they are aligned on what steps they need to take. The importance of building strong relationships and alliances cannot be overstated since this will ensure the maintenance of mental equilibrium and a very valuable sense of solidarity and mutual support at a particularly difficult time.

Solutions to be considered will include, in order of priority:

i) Take the matter up with the head of HR (if they exist and are of sufficient seniority and wisdom to be of support).

ii) Go as a team to Martin and explain clearly to him how they see the present situation. Bring proposals/solutions that have been properly thought through and jointly agreed by the team. This is to *focus on solutions* (*6*), but also entails *setting boundaries* (*4*) and *being assertive* (*5*). *Staying calm* (*3*) is essential, especially when negotiating with Martin and any other company executives who need to be informed.

iii) Take the discussion upwards to the next level of management should the discussion with Martin not result in an agreed plan of action (and the removal of threats). Again, a high level of maturity is required to do this well, applying *Key Strategies 3*, *4*, *5*, and *6* while constantly *building great relationships* (*7*). If this is done well and the proposals make sense and are properly workable, it will be very difficult for the next level of management to turn the plan down. They would risk losing an entire team in the process. Any enlightened leader would be very unwise not to listen very carefully to what the team say.

Conclusion: Leadership in Business

Prospective leaders may or may not have some innate natural abilities and qualities and they may have had opportunities (for example, in sports) to demonstrate these. But there is a world of difference between someone with *some* skills in leadership and a seasoned leader. It is like the difference in the sporting world between an amateur, however talented, and a professional.

In this case study, Martin has not grown sufficiently in his previous positions nor been given the level of leadership training needed to carry out this awesome responsibility. The person who appointed Martin into such a position is clearly also suspect, as is the company that is so obviously devoid of proper processes for agreeing promotions.

In the absence of a proper process, appointments will tend to be made too quickly. Managers will naturally be more comfortable with people who are most like themselves. This can often prevent the creation of a balanced team with some breadth of experience and perspective.

There is no magic formula. It requires maturity and intelligent reflection, accompanied interviewers with proper training and a real understanding of the requirements of the role. This seems very obvious. And it is. However, it is often difficult to put into practice. Appropriate training is very often dismissed, while off-the-cuff decisions are made too frequently in the interests of speed and expediency.

29

The Toxic Employee

Case Study F

Key Strategies: Know who you are (2), be assertive (5), focus on solutions (6), build great relationships (7)

Background

Brendan joined the consulting company shortly after finishing his doctorate in business administration. After a nine-month induction and training period, he joined the finance and business strategy department. His role was as a business analyst with responsibility for investigating and analysing acquisitions. Some of the acquisitions emanated from the consulting company itself (who were looking out for possible candidates of interest to their clients) and some were specifically requested to be analysed by a client.

Brendan reported to Naomi (the head of one of several groups of analysts) and she, along with the other group heads, reported to the divisional head of the business strategy department, Mary. Mary worked closely with the finance team and with the lead client partner, who had direct and permanent contact with the client and responsibility for the project outcome.

When projects arose, Mary would decide with the analyst group heads which team should take the assignment. Most often this would be done on the basis of previous client experience and workloads. Sometimes a client would request a particular person or team if they had worked with them before.

The department worked flexibly, with analysts often working in a different group if circumstances required. They also liaised closely with the finance team and with the client lead partner. It was generally expected that analysts and group heads worked longer hours and during weekends at critical times, especially when acquisitions were nearing completion.

Brendan was welcomed into Naomi's group (not least since it was short staffed) and familiarised himself rapidly with the work and with his new environment. It was obvious that he was talented and a quick learner and would be able to contribute rapidly to the group's assignments. He was also ambitious and keen to show that he was fully up to the role.

His first assignments went well. His inputs were welcomed and appreciated. Naomi was pleased with his work and told him so. She also told Mary that Brendan had made a great start.

Brendan was given more challenging assignments, which he again accomplished well. However, in the process of carrying out the work, he did start to insinuate that he felt he was contributing more than several of his colleagues and that he felt his work was of higher quality.

During the course of one presentation, he began to interrupt and take over some of the discussion with his personal interpretation of the acquisition and its viability. He directed his comments very deliberately at Mary—bypassing both his colleagues and Naomi.

His points were all perfectly good and he was obviously very competent with an instinctive ability to rapidly get to the key issues of projects. But many of his ideas had in fact been put forward by *other* members of the group during their weekly reviews. However, Brendan gave them no credit—implying that he was the one to have come up with them.

In the office, he began making occasional offhand and mildly cynical comments about the performance of the department. He thought it was rather slow paced and lacked insightful critique when assessing projects. He suggested a number of improvements that could be made—implying that some of these seemed fairly obvious to him.

Mary, who witnessed his performance in the presentations, was clearly impressed by his obvious technical competence and listened carefully to his inputs. Naomi also valued his thoughts and ideas, many of which she welcomed and felt to be valid and perspicacious. She was fully prepared to adopt those she felt were most appropriate. She could see Brendan was extremely bright and could have a very fine future. He was capable of adding many refreshing ideas to the department and to the projects. Here was a star in the making.

But Naomi was also troubled. Contrary to Brandan's somewhat overinflated expectations, she saw that not all of his ideas were implementable. Much more importantly, she was very conscious that her department's harmony was being unsettled by his poor interpersonal skills. She was increasingly concerned that the teamwork that was such a strong feature of the group was being eroded by Brendan's toxic behaviour. If it continued (or worsened), it would become highly detrimental to the group's effectiveness.

Naomi knew that her group performed best when the team members operated harmoniously together. This meant a relaxed and tension-free environment, where egos were left at the door and all team members were respected. Put-downs were not accepted and would be openly called out whenever they happened. (The team had once agreed to leave a basket on the centre of the table and levy a $1 fine on any team member making a putdown. After an hour, the exercise was stopped as members had run out of money! But the lesson had been learnt and team cohesion had been enhanced.) In the spirit of openness, team members would bounce ideas off each other and collectively arrive at solutions. This worked well and Naomi recognized that the solutions and opinions proposed by the team transcended the ability of any one of them singly. However brilliant Brendan might be, the cohesion of the team was much more important.

Things came to a head when a new urgent project came to the department. Naomi asked for volunteers to work Friday evening and over the weekend. What normally happened would be that two or three of those who regularly worked together and had few family commitments would volunteer. Brendan, who had no family or other commitments, volunteered. No one, however, offered to or wanted to partner with him. In a pique of barely suppressed anger, Brendan said to Naomi in front of the group that he had changed his mind. He would not put himself forward either for this project or any future weekend work!

How to manage a toxic employee using Key Strategies

It is a regrettable that our education systems are based more on individual achievements as opposed to collective teamwork. Hardly any formal education is devoted to leadership, interpersonal, listening, empathy, relationship building or other EQ skills. As a result, students often lack any proper self-awareness. Because they are praised for their academic abilities, they often lack humility and believe themselves to be much better than they are. Unfortunately, nobody has told them otherwise—to their detriment.

They grow up somewhat deluded and tend to develop an entitlement attitude. This mixture is highly toxic.

What Naomi is facing is not uncommon. It is found in the business world and any industry or sporting environment where talented individuals are much in demand but have to learn to work in teams. What Naomi needs to achieve is to retain Brendan while preserving the harmony and effectiveness of her team. She must address his toxicity as soon as possible and before it causes greater problems.

Key Strategy 1, keep away, is not appropriate now that Brendan has been recruited. (Although, if attempts to remedy the situation are not successful, 'keep away' will have to become 'keep *him* away'—either through transfer or termination.)

Key Strategy 2, know who you are, remains essential for Naomi as she addresses Brendan in the right way. She has to maintain her composure, being completely comfortable about her responsibility to speak to him and acting from a position of psychological comfort. She will also need to *keep calm* (*3*) when dealing with Brendan while maintaining the cohesion of her team and when explaining her proposed action plan to Mary, which she must do first. It is essential that Mary, as her boss, understands, accepts and supports her proposals before going further.

The most important advice in this context is to *be assertive* (5). Once Mary is on side, Naomi will need to discuss the situation face to face with Brendan and be assertive throughout the interview. She will need to speak clearly to Brendan, without embarrassment or aggression. She must explain that while everyone acknowledges his evident talents (and great potential future), he will only be able to work in her department as *part of the team* and not as a lone star.

She has to make clear to him that this requirement is non-negotiable and that her observation of his behaviour has necessitated such a discussion. If necessary, and this is highly likely, she should go into specific detail and explain clearly how each of his interventions has been disruptive and caused disquiet. There is no room here for any compromise. Brendan's behaviour must change. He has to: understand the seriousness of the situation; accept it; and want to do something about it.

This may not be an easy session. Brendan is unlikely to be aware of the seriousness of the situation—since his self-awareness level is not high. Naomi will have to be sufficiently resilient, self-confident and determined (*Key Strategy 2*) to persuade Brendan that there is work for him to do if he is to unlock his real potential.

Once Brendan accepts that he has to learn and grow, Naomi can move on to *Key Strategy 6, focus on solutions.* Brendan would benefit from a full EQ Assessment, in which his emotional competences are evaluated and reported back to him and to Naomi. This assessment will include skills such as self-perception and awareness, emotional expression and assertiveness, interpersonal relationships and empathy, decision-taking and stress management. The data provided by Brendan himself in completing the diagnostic will enable a detailed discussion of which areas Brendan should focus on and which subsequent programs he should follow. It will also allow the company and Naomi to track Brendan's progress as he applies his learning to his rehabilitation within the team.

Naomi should discuss the suggested solutions with the team (with Brendan's agreement) so that team members can help and guide Brendan through this next stage. The team members are already competent team players and work harmoniously together. They will be able to help Brendan learn and grow—if he has the good sense to ask them. Brendan will then have the opportunity to apply *Key Strategy 7, build great relationships.* He can forge friendships and connections that, when correctly established for mutual benefit, can last a lifetime. They will provide countless opportunities for learning, as well as avoiding costly mistakes.

Ultimately, however, it is up to Brendan to make the decision. He has to take responsibility and grasp this opportunity with openness, enthusiasm and enjoyment. It is up to Brendan to change.

> It is not the strongest of the species that survive, nor the most intelligent, but the one most responsive to change.
>
> —Leon C Megginson,
> summarising Charles Darwin

30

The Toxic Parent

Case Study G

Key Strategies: Set boundaries (4) and be assertive (5)

Background

Andrew's mother, Geraldine, now in her eighties and living in her own flat, was always the woman in charge of the household. As a young married mother of two and with a husband at work six days a week, it was left to her to manage the home and children. Life was tough. There were frequent shortages, clothes needed to be mended and food carefully shared. There was no time for leisure, and everyone had their task to attend to.

Geraldine had been brought up in a similar way. Her own father was always at work and her mother, Victoria, had ruled with a rod of iron. Only Geraldine had six siblings! Although Victoria was very fond and proud of her seven children, there was never any time for shows of affection or love—let alone to pander to any 'fusses'. Nor did she allow any of her children to question or complain. Children were to be seen and not heard. They grew up used to being told what to do and how to do it. Having experienced what would happen if they disagreed with anything—namely a heavy smack—they rapidly learned to comply.

As a result, the household was a generally peaceful one, but utterly devoid of laughter, fun or happiness. When Geraldine's mum reached her eighties, her family were still living at home. It was expected that they would look after her, which they did. Until the day she died.

Geraldine had continued the family 'tradition' and governed strictly. She frightened the children and her own husband with her aggression and would criticize and harangue them until she got her own way. It was a case of 'my way or no way' and no one dared challenge her. She controlled by bullying and threatening.

Andrew's father, George, spent more and more time away. When he was at home, he was stressed and unhappy. He was clearly at odds with his wife on many subjects but too fearful of the response he would receive to argue back. He soldiered on for several years and then died of a stroke.

Andrew did well at school and wanted to go into the army, where he felt he would receive a good education as well as some adventure. Above all, he would be away from home. His mother objected and organised with the family doctor for him to be disqualified on the grounds of poor health. She was frightened for her son and wanted him to pursue a different career. Andrew's father had been in the oil and gas industry, and she wanted Andrew to get a degree in chemical or mechanical engineering and follow the same career. There were heated arguments but, eventually, Geraldine won.

Andrew went to university to study chemical engineering, having passed his maths and science subjects with flying colours. From the moment he set foot in the university, he hated it. He found the teachers were cold and unfriendly and their lectures lacked enthusiasm. The city was dull and dangerous, with frequent muggings. He made friends and they kept together and helped each other. But none of them enjoyed the experience at all.

Andrew was now in his late teens and had had a year away from home. He knew that a career in oil and gas was not for him. And he still wanted to join the army. He contacted his doctor and asked to be retested, as he thought that the condition that had disqualified him initially was no longer valid. He was right. His doctor gave him a clean bill of health. In reality, there had never been anything wrong with him. He had always been strong, energetic and healthy.

Andrew dropped out of university, applied to join the army and was accepted. He now came home to tell his mother about his decision! She was outraged, not only by Andrew's decision, which she considered foolhardy, but also because he had not consulted her first—nor told her about his visit to the doctor. She said she felt utterly betrayed. She was bewildered. She told him that he did not appreciate all that she had done for him and that he was an ungrateful and selfish child. She refused to speak to him for several days and continued haranguing him in the hope that he might change his mind. He did not.

Andrew joined the army and received a competent education. Although it was a tough time, the camaraderie was motivating and he made friends easily. He took the option to leave at the end of his first term of duty and decided to pursue his own career. He went to a different and more prestigious university and studied business administration. He thoroughly enjoyed his time, made many friends and met a young woman, Elise, who subsequently became his wife and with whom he had four children.

Andrew's mother, Geraldine remained unhappy and highly negative about his choices. She was relieved that nothing untoward had happened during his military service but did not approve of Andrew's choice of business administration, which she felt was not a 'proper occupation'. Above all, she did not approve of Elise.

Andrew decided the family should move abroad—in spite of Geraldine's protestations of being abandoned. Geraldine developed a number of illnesses, including back pain, high blood pressure, panic attacks and type 2 diabetes. Her asthma also worsened and was particularly intense in times of stress. Geraldine pleaded with Andrew either to come back or to have her go to live with him and his family. She told him that her dream was to be the lovely old granny surrounded by her child and grandchildren She also told him that his cruelty was killing her.

Andrew refused. He knew his wife and children would be deeply unhappy as his mother would revert to her controlling and bullying ways. Instead, he ensured that she lived comfortably in a pleasant flat, had access to private care and carers to come to look after her. He paid for everything. She continued to complain and there were regular disagreements. But he and his family remained resolute. His family came first.

Assessing the Key Strategies used for managing a toxic parent

It is regrettably almost always the case that we repeat the customs and practices of our parents. Parents are the first people we depend on. We love and admire them and they are our first teachers. Unfortunately, parents are not taught how to be good parents.

Sure, they will protect, feed and clothe their children, but they generally have no idea how to attend to the psychological and emotional needs of their children.

In the absence of proper knowledge, they tend to copy what their parents did. What else do they know? If the parents were strict, they are strict. If laissez-faire, they are laissez-faire. If they are traditional, they will encourage boys to be strong and self-sufficient and girls to be gentle and more accommodating. While this is evolving (often rapidly) in some parts of the world and in some households, it is still very prevalent in the majority of countries.

This is hardly surprising as there is no formal education about parenting, and what there is does not address emotional or psychological issues. The blind continue to lead the blind. The 'shadow' of the parent falls on the child. The child-self is crushed as the infant joins the adult world. The love that the child so surely wants and needs is absent. Society conditions the child to its controlling needs. History repeats itself and will continue to repeat itself until the shadow and the child-self emotional and psychological needs have been confronted and addressed. This can be through education and understanding. Or, as in this case study, through the conscious determination to change.

Andrew understood what was happening and determined to move away. In terms of Key Strategies, he was adopting *Key Strategy 1, recognize toxicity and avoid.* He resolved to do so, whatever the pressure on him. He was convinced, not only that this was the right course, but also that he absolutely did not want to repeat this history with his own family. He deliberately chose a very different course for his life.

As time passed and Andrew thought through what he wanted and his options, he gradually became aware of who he really was—*Key Strategy 2, master yourself, know who you are*. He knew very clearly what he did *not* want first. He then proceeded to discover what he *did* want and pursued those goals. His friendships, and then meeting Elise, rekindled his natural kindness and compassion.

His love for his family included a deep caring for the emotional and psychological needs of his children. Without formal teaching on parenting, or indeed a conscious or intellectual understanding of what was happening in his own mind, his natural gentleness and kindness allowed him to tap into his true self.

Parenting, nurturing, helping, teaching, guiding and healing are never intellectual exercises. They are emotional responses that come naturally to the empathetic soul. These values and virtues cannot really be acquired. They can only happen when the spirit is open, aware, receptive and present.

Key Strategy 2, know who you are, was also invaluable to Andrew in realising that his mother's accusations of selfishness (and abandonment) were projections of her own state of mind. Parents can often become attached to their children in an unhealthy way. This attachment becomes obsessive and is no longer based on love but on fear—the work of ego.

Parents are frightened to let go, frightened of being lonely, frightened of empty nest syndrome. They have become so attached to the concept of being a (dominant) parent that when that role dies, they too die. Learning to let go when the time comes is an act of pure love. And the wonderful thing is that, in letting go, the parents transition into a new phase of life. And then the children they have let go, keep wanting to come back.

This appears to be paradoxical, but is a reflection of a universal truth. This truth is expressed as 'What goes around comes around,' and 'We reap what we sow.' This is the law of cause and effect, also known as the law of karma. It is universal and immutable!

For the other Key Strategies, Andrew learned *stay calm* (*3*) regularly in his discussions with his mother. The army had instilled this necessary virtue and he was able to use it effectively. He avoided being triggered by her various tactics, tantrums and the emotional blackmail she used to try to control him.

In managing his mother, Andrew was able to *set boundaries* (*4*) and *be assertive* (*5*) and kept to his position through the barrage of objections. By setting boundaries, he resolved not to accept anything that would affect the happiness and harmony of his own family. He also knew to *look for solutions* (*6*), which for him meant providing the most comfortable environment for his mother and helping to find her the best possible care for her ailments. He also visited whenever he could.

Finally, using *Key Strategy 7, build great relationships*, with his friends, wife and family, allowed him to think through, calmly and carefully, what was right for them and for him.

Andrew began life with many difficulties and constraints. He was brought up in a generally inimical environment in which he was bullied and browbeaten. He learned to surmount all of these through his own will and determination. In his most difficult dealings, and without conscious knowledge, he applied all the Key Strategies we are recommending.

31

The Toxic Friendship

Case Study H

Key Strategies: Know who you are (2), set boundaries (4) and build great relationships (7)

Background

Patricia and Claire had known each other for several years. They were both in their late thirties and had many similar interests. They enjoyed time out together, going to restaurants, events and clubs and occasional shopping trips. They had mutual friends and enjoyed meeting up together in a social setting.

They divorced at around the same time and had shared custody of their children. They both had a teenage son and daughter. During their painful and lengthy divorce processes, they had supported each other.

Patricia's husband, Steve, was a very traditionally minded and serious small business owner. Before the divorce, he expected his wife to stay at home and look after the children. On the other hand, Claire's husband, David, was a freelance consultant and financial adviser who expected his wife to find lucrative employment in order to contribute financially to the family coffers.

Steve and David were both rather introverted, cold and rigid. After their children were born, the men went back to work immediately and left their wives to fend for themselves. The women felt neglected, unloved and unsupported. Steve was always busy at work and lacked warmth and love. David spent his time working on questionable financial projects that seemed to promise much but never delivered.

At home, Steve devoted his time exclusively to the children, who he worshipped, but he ignored Patricia. It was almost as if he was competing with her for the children's attention. David tended to be depressed and dysfunctional, leaving the parental tasks to Claire; from time to time, he would disappear in a dark mood.

Patricia continually wanted to develop herself, take courses and study subjects she had never had the opportunity to pursue growing up. She wanted to find a suitable career and set up her own business, separate from Steve. She was devoted to her children and encouraged them to find their own destiny and follow subjects that they enjoyed.

Claire was happy enough to find employment and look after the children at home,but she was looking for a more exciting life than the one she had with David, as well as an easier one, and wished her husband could be more dynamic and motivated. She was extroverted, always the heart and soul of a party.

Patricia and Steve's different expectations and perspectives on life—as well as their often difficult, conflict-ridden communication and frequent rows—resulted in their decision to divorce.

Claire's enthusiasm for excitement and change was similarly at odds with husband David's restrained and introverted temperament: they were frustrated with each other. David had an affair.

Claire followed with one of her own. It was clear that the marriage was irretrievably broken. They too decided to divorce.

Both divorces took a long time to complete and were messy, unhappy affairs. The women, however, quickly found new boyfriends and went out together as they had done before. When the boyfriends failed to live up to expectations, they were soon replaced.

Meanwhile, Patricia and Claire's friendship was beginning to change. Perhaps the friendship was never as deep or sustainable as they had thought. Differences emerged. Claire expected Patricia to participate in every occasion she organised and was disappointed when the latter turned her down or left early.

Patricia continued to spend her time developing her newfound skills and interests. She found the parties and social occasions increasingly tiresome, where time and again, the same discussions repeated themselves and the conversation was largely gossip—much of it critical, unkind and unwarranted. She also noticed that Claire craved excitement and was befriending new like-minded souls.

Claire's boyfriend, though absent much of the time, was relatively welloff, which encouraged her to be increasingly and visibly extravagant. Patricia liked nice things too, but her nature was more reserved and discreet. The women went on holiday together with the children (not the boyfriends), and the differences between them were ever more obvious. Claire wanted to find babysitters so they could go out and party, while Patricia preferred to spend time exploring and visiting with her children. Claire was not concerned about being on time for anyone; Pat was more disciplined.

When in town, Claire was often loud to the point of rudeness. Patricia, on the other hand, showed people respect and compassion—she would never raise her voice and she found it brash to do so. She thought Claire was losing all sense of propriety and was becoming boorish. Meanwhile, her proper behaviour irritated Claire, who would urge her to get more of a life, let go of her hang-ups and just have some fun. Claire thought that Patricia was becoming too self-absorbed and boring, and even that joy was disappearing from the relationship.

Yet Claire would still always turn to Patricia for help. She was often distraught because she was desperate for her boyfriend to marry her while he would present every possible reason to delay, sending her into floods of tears, drama and panic attacks. Patricia would drop what she was doing to support Claire through her traumas. Then, Claire would return to her rambunctious ways—until the next occasion.

When Patricia started to have boyfriend difficulties, Claire was dismissive. She urged her friend to come off the phone, pull herself together and join her with whatever activity she wanted to indulge in.

Claire and Patricia's circles of friends changed. Claire sought wealthier, more extravagant friends, while Pat gravitated towards more socially and globally conscious people who had a deeper sense of responsibility and compassion.

It was clear that the friendship had deteriorated. Every conversation became a dance. Each tried to avoid upsetting the other, yet they offended one another, and both were unhappy and unsatisfied with each other. Neither wished to address the matter directly for fear of the consequence. The relationship had become toxic.

How to use Key Strategies to avoid a relationship becoming toxic

We all evolve and mature at different paces. The things that entertained and amused us at one age, may seem trivial and mindless at another. Relationships evolve too. As we grow and develop and become conscious of who we really are, the relationships that were once fulfilling may grow stale, disappoint and then irritate. If it becomes obvious that a relationship is 'asymmetric' (one party feels they are always giving while the other is always taking), then the relationship is heading for trouble.

In this case study, the central issue is that Patricia has evolved and grown in maturity more rapidly than Claire. Patricia has started to apply *Key Strategy 2, know who you are*, to herself and has found that she is no longer satisfied with a life of mindless hedonism and frivolity. Yes, going out and occasional shopping excursions are fun, but not as a way of life. Overt exhibitions of wealth, brashness that verges on rudeness, emotional demands and drama have become tiresome to Patricia. She has moved on. She has let go of that phase of her life.

What matters to Patricia now has radically changed, while Claire's priorities have remained largely unchanged. That happens even if no value judgments are intended (but often arise in fact).

We are all different and differences should be respected. What is important, is that the implications and consequences should also be equally well understood and accepted.

There are times when it is best to leave whatever no longer serves us. With friends, we can find new, more aligned people with whom we can share joy in a relaxed, non-judgmental and ego-free environment. It is only by abandoning the old and welcoming the new that we can continue to grow in wisdom and understanding. To stay locked in the present relationship is to accept being stuck in a psychological quagmire.

Inevitably, this realization brings us to adopt *Key Strategy 1, keep your distance*. In this case, it would mean for Patricia to reduce contact with Claire substantially, avoid being drawn into her toxic-induced dramas and to find a new environment in which to grow and find meaning.

Key Strategy 4, set clear boundaries, will apply, for certain, but principally to ourselves. We need to be very awake to the risks of going backwards. We should not allow ourselves to be drawn back into the previous toxic situation.

Key Strategy 7, build great relationships also applies, but there are two aspects to it. First, the previous relationship, while no longer right, must not be destroyed. It has represented an important period in the life of both parties, in which there were tears but also great joy. This is a cause for celebration and due reverence. Now the relationship is no longer comfortable or appropriate. Both parties have to gently agree—either tacitly or if possible consciously—to let it drift away. The objective is to avoid any sense of resentment, anger or grief. Both individuals need to move on in peace and without any residual stress or tension.

Secondly, new relationships need to be built—using the learnings from the previous experience. Life is an opportunity for continuous, mind-and-soul expanding learning and personal growth. The greater the realization of who we truly are, the more we find new eyes to discover new landscapes, new truths, new joys, new relationships. We find we are beyond the conditioned ego and the triviality of unreal 'things' that dissolve. We find what is genuinely real, what never changes and is eternal.

There is real and awesome magic in the cooperation and collaboration of like-minded people who share common ideals and intentions and whose conscious awareness is evolving on a similar wavelength and with similar vibrations. Any relaxed, ego-free environment, in which people feel safe, respected and encouraged, will always stimulate the greatest personal growth and the most inspiring creativity.

Relationships evolve and change and that is just how it is. The key is to recognize when enough is enough and when moving on is the best policy for all.

Moving on in a compassionate and loving way will always be best. Tomorrow is another day. We only have one short life, and it is an extraordinary gift. When we are given a gift, we should be grateful for it and take good care of it. It should not be taken for granted or squandered stressfully or toxically. Rather, it should be embraced—fully and completely. This means growing in consciousness and purpose. After all, why else are we here?

Appendix 1

The Importance and Value of Meditation

Understand the self, reduce stress and find peace

Throughout Toxicum, we have stressed the necessity of increasing self-awareness. It is one of the keys to managing toxicity. There are various ways to do this, but we have found that one of the most effective is through quiet reflection and meditation.

Meditation is the art of being silent and quiet. As such, it is something that is often very difficult for people living harried lives. Yet it is the gateway to reducing stress by discovering true inner peace and connecting to who we really are. *Discovering who we truly are at the deepest level* may seem like an esoteric concept, but it is the key to injecting some reality into our unreal perceptions and assumptions. It blows away the superficiality of our otherwise cluttered, frantic and meaningless existence.

Without meditation (the ability to sit quietly with ourselves in gentle contemplation), we condemn ourselves to a life of stress and anxiety, sleepless nights and poor health prospects. Without it, we are victim to the incessant stream of thoughts that constantly plague us.

Meditation does not need to be complicated or lengthy. There is no necessity to sit in uncomfortable positions or to try desperately to empty the mind with eyes closed while at the same time trying to focus on esoteric breathing techniques. That is not meditation!

Meditation can be practised at any time and anywhere. Walking meditation in nature works well. Sitting still and quietly, even in a crowded place, is fine. The key is to allow whatever is happening to happen—without judgment or interference. Let any noises just waft through.

Breathing is very important. Focus on the breath and allow the diaphragm rather than the stomach to do the work. Breathe slowly and evenly, without force. If you are able, close the eyes (obviously not with walking meditation!). This will reduce distractions. As you focus on the breath and keep rhythmical and 'joined', extraneous thoughts will gradually disappear. If thoughts re-enter the mind, let them pass by and then focus on the breath again. Allow the same to happen with any sounds. Music and mantras can also be very helpful.

It is perfectly alright to meditate with eyes open. If the eyes are open, allow them to soften… and smile gently.

The key is to actively surrender by accepting and welcoming everything. Engage with the reality of the present moment, the moment that is being experienced right now. And let it sink in. Stay present and aware. And let everything just go. It is what it is. You are what you are. We find this practice echoed in one of the four 'Great Sayings' of the ancient Hindu texts, the Upanishads: *Tat Tvam Asi*, which means 'Thou art That.'

It is no accident that Nirvana, in Sanskrit, means 'blowing out'—the sound and feeling that occurs when we breathe out deeply. It is the sound of relief and acceptance. We relax on the outbreath. We go to sleep on the outbreath. Meditation is a natural and easy practice.

When Westerners first visit a temple, they tend to ask the priest what he is meditating 'on'. He will look surprised and answer: 'We don't meditate on anything. We just meditate.'

Meditation has many well-researched benefits to mental and physical health including:

1. reduction of stress, anxiety and depression;
2. decreased blood pressure;
3. decreased chronic pain;
4. improved attention span and memory;
5. improved sleep;
6. enhanced feelings of kindness and acceptance towards others;
7. improved interactions with others;
8. greater understanding and acceptance of the self;
9. recognition and replacement of thoughts that may be harmful or self-defeating with positive thoughts;
10. increased problem-solving skills;
11. improved mood;
12. improved decision-making;
13. improved self-awareness;
14. dilution of ego.

By garnering these benefits, toxicity automatically reduces. When toxicity subsides, it means the ego has subsided too. When ego subsides, openness and conscious awareness happen. Then positive change is able to occur.

When any ego-derived structure dissolves it will, initially, cause suffering and pain. Paradoxically, it will also open the door to self-awareness. It is an awakening to our truth that allows the light to shine in and expose the toxicity in our lives. Once exposed to the light (which means confronted actively and courageously), toxicity loses its power and ceases to be. The wounds that we have lived with all these years, which have dominated our reactions and our projections, can now begin to heal. We have discovered the secret of living a real and authentic life.

Appendix 2

Quick Checklist for Toxic Emergencies

The Key Strategies at a glance

This checklist is designed to be a rapid reminder of *Toxicum*'s Key Strategies and how to use them should a toxic circumstance presents itself.

1. Avoid toxicity

Whenever you *feel* in any way uncomfortable with a person who shows toxic tendencies, your body instinct will almost certainly be correct.

Keep and stay away if you can.

In the early stages of a relationship, guard your personal information. Do not disclose income details. And do not lend money.

Do not allow harassment or violence of any sort.

If you cannot keep away for good, specific reasons (such as with a family member) follow the other Key Strategies.

> If you walked away from a toxic, negative, abusive,
> one-sided, dead-end, low vibrational relationship or
> friendship—you won.
>
> —Lalah Delia

2. Know who you are

Stay in your power at all times. Do not give it away. You always have a choice. We create our own reality. We have the power to say yes or no.

Happiness is a choice, not a result. So is misery. Know what you want and who you really are.

Be comfortable in your skin and have confidence in your instincts. Remind yourself at all times that:

I am the master of my fate
I am the captain of my soul.

—William Ernest Henley, 'Invictus'

3. Keep calm

The ability to remain calm when all around are losing their heads is the hallmark of maturity. It is a clear indication of someone truly in control of their emotions and who knows who they are. It is also an essential quality of leadership.

Staying calm requires you to understand the difference between reacting and responding.

Re-acting is the automatic knee-jerk backlash of ego. When ego feels it is being aggressed, it fights to protect itself—with whatever weapon it can find.

Responding emanates from consciousness and presence. It is an expression of understanding and empathy. Staying calm and saying nothing is often the best strategy. Do not try to defend, attack, deny, blame or criticize—these are all the function of ego. Stay silent and calm. The storm will blow itself out and your calm will establish a platform for moving forward without drama.

> Calmness of mind does not mean you should stop your activity. Real calmness should be found in activity itself. We say, 'It is easy to have calmness in inactivity, it is hard to have calmness in activity, but calmness in activity is true calmness.'
>
> —Shunryu Suzuki,
> *Zen Mind, Beginner's Mind*

4. Set boundaries

You have the right to lay out your own boundaries. This applies to yourself (what you are prepared to do and not do) as well as to the other person. Set clear boundaries (for example, do not text or call me outside our scheduled agreement) and specific consequences if these are broken (I will no longer help you and will not answer your calls.)

Once you have established a boundary, keep to it. It will be counterproductive and damaging to self-worth and credibility to give way. For example, if the person texts or tries to call outside the agreed schedule, do not answer the phone or reply to the text and, if necessary, block the caller.

> Your personal boundaries protect the inner core of your identity and your right to choices.
>
> —David Richo

5. Be assertive

Assertiveness is a critically important skill in managing toxicity. It is the ability to communicate clearly and unambiguously, without shame or aggression, while being sensitive to the feelings of others and understanding their responses.

Assertiveness depends on several factors:

- the degree to which we have sufficient self-awareness to recognize our triggers, know who we are and be truthful;
- the skill with which we are able to express our feelings, even disapproval and annoyance, without losing control;
- the ability we have to stand up for our rights and to disagree, while not ignoring other people's beliefs or resorting to disruptive emotional mischief;
- the capacity we have for finding win-win solutions, thereby strengthening rather than weakening the bonds of relationships.

Before engaging with anyone, it is wise to listen carefully to the words of others and then ask yourself four simple questions:

Is it true?
Is it kind?
Is it necessary?
Is it helpful?

If the answer to all of these is yes, then it is right to say what we have to say without passivity or aggression.

> To be passive is to let others decide for you. To be aggressive is to decide for others. To be assertive is to decide for yourself. And to trust that there is enough. That you are enough.
>
> —Edith Eva Eger

6. Focus on solutions

Once the time is right in a toxic situation, move the conversation towards finding solutions. For example, if a toxic person complains, criticizes or judges, allow them a little time to calm down, then ask them:

- what they would do;
- how they would respond;
- what they consider would be the best course of action.

Shifting from a negative to a positive perspective encourages the mind to be more constructive. In a work situation, asking this question will result in a discussion. Often, the outcome is a (tacit) agreement that the course of action that caused the toxic reaction is actually the best. And if a better one is found, so much the better! The engagement of the toxic person in the process is key to finding win-win solutions.

> Sometimes the situation is only a problem because it is looked at in a certain way. Looked at in another way, the right course of action may be so obvious that the problem no longer exists.
>
> —Edward de Bono

7. Build great relationships

In any toxic emergency, call a trusted friend or a family member. True friends will always be there for you. They will help by providing objectivity, empathy, understanding and kindness. True friends do not judge. They support and defend you and guide you in your decision-making at these critical moments.

Choose your friends with care. Know who will be right there with you and provide unconditional support when things are difficult. Know who you can count on. Such friends are pure gold.

Build such relationships, mend them when necessary and nurture them always. You are not separate. Develop powerful connections. This is the magic of Oneness.

> Building and repairing relationships are long-term investments.
>
> —Stephen Covey

Acknowledgements

Our thanks go to the many people who, directly or indirectly, have contributed to this book. Some inspired us with their ancient wisdom and philosophies. Some, such as our families and friends, have advised and supported us with kindness and patience throughout a fairly long process. Yet others have contributed inadvertently and anonymously by their behaviours and actions which we have been able to observe and include in the 'case studies' that illustrate the strategies.

Because many of the ideas and strategies of Toxicum are based on the teachings of the *Way: Finding Peace in Turbulent Times* which itself owes so much to the wisdom of highly respected Eastern and Western sages, philosophers and psychologists, our thanks are due to such luminaries as the incomparable Lao Tzu, Carl Jung, Albert Einstein, Epictetus, Marcus Aurelius, and Zen masters such as Dogen and Shunryu Suzuki, as well as modern thinkers such as Alan watts, Wayne Dyer, Eckhart Tolle, John Covey, Michael Brown and many others. They inspire our thinking every day.

Toxicum contains elements of Jungian psychology, especially as regards the 'shadow work'. This is distilled from the work of Carl Jung as well as his many followers. We are indebted to Carl Jung and his critics in particular for helping to provide the substance for the sections on understanding our own toxicity, essential if we are to manage the toxicity of others.

Many thanks go to Prof Bud Drago and his wife Angela for their always helpful and enthusiastic comments and suggestions and to Jean Fleming for her contributions to our deeper understanding of toxicity in the workplace. Thanks also go to Casper Jaarsma for his very accurate proofreading as well as his erudite comments.

And of course we are very grateful for the superb work of our editor, Jill Ronsley, and her outstanding contributions to this book. It is always a great pleasure to work with someone who has the sensitivity and intellect to grasp all the essential features of our work as well as the artistic talent to represent them in such an elegant and attractive manner. Her many suggestions and ideas have been extremely welcome.

About the Authors

Vernon Sankey

Vernon Sankey was born in France and educated in the UK. He graduated in Modern Languages at Oriel College, Oxford. He went from university into industry, where he spent the next 28 years in various countries, culminating as chief executive of a major international corporation in the UK.

He then became a non-executive director and chairman of several large and small international companies and is still active in this field today. During and since this time he has lectured and run courses on leadership, motivation and stress management in corporations, business conferences, universities, and schools.

In 1999 he co-founded a coaching and mentoring company where he further developed his knowledge of Cognitive Psychology and NLP to help mentor business executives as well as people in all walks of life. He has since studied and is proficient in Hypnotherapy and EQ Assessment which complement his coaching, mentoring and counselling skills.

Vernon's first publication was *The Stairway to Happiness* (2018) followed by *The Way: Finding Peace in Turbulent Times* (2019) and

The Way Workbook (2021) co-authored with Katey Lockwood. *Toxicum* is Vernon's fourth book and the third co-authored with Katey, with whom he also founded www.improvemyworld.com

Vernon is married with four children and eight grandchildren and lives in Berkshire.

Katey Lockwood

Katey Lockwood is a Personal Transformation Coach and Spiritual Teacher.

Katey's personal development skills together with her NLP practitioner background and her knowledge of Cognitive Psychology create a unique platform for supporting businesses and helping individuals. She is also qualified to perform Emotional Intelligence assessments using psychometric tests (e.g. EQi-2.0 and 360) and Hypnotherapy.

Her personal approach is based on two, life transforming principles: 'Know Thyself' and 'Be the change in the world you want to be.' Guiding her clients to work introspectively and to discover their true purpose, she helps them find a happier and more effective way of conducting their life and career.

Katey's clients include business executives, well-known celebrities, sports people, and people in many different professions wanting to make changes in their life. She also does voluntary coaching, helping members of the public and friends.

Katey has also been a Trustee of the Katie Piper foundation, whose vision is to have a world where scars do not limit a person's function, social inclusion, or sense of wellbeing. She worked extensively with Katie herself.

Katey studied Philosophy at The London School of Economics and has attended numerous courses. Her previous career was in media, during which she has been a model, an actress and on the Harry Potter special effects team.

Katey has been working with Vernon Sankey for several years and is the co-founder of improvemyworld.com. She has taken part with him in podcasts, video interviews, national and international workshops, and corporate courses, covering stress management, life skills, leadership, and personal transformation.

In 2019, she co-authored a book with him called *The Way: Finding Peace in Turbulent Times* and, in 2021, they published another book entitled *The Way Workbook,* which is a modular course for managing stress and living a more effective and happier life, based on the learnings of *The Way: Finding Peace in Turbulent Times. Toxicum* is their third book.

Katey is an active gym and yoga practitioner and lives in Buckinghamshire, UK with her daughter.

Printed in Great Britain
by Amazon

10773461R00149